STO

ALLEN COUNTY PUBLIC LIBRARY

3 18

FRIENDS
OF ACPL

j797
Coombs, Charles
Soaring: Where Hawks and Eagles
Fly

LC 8-19-05

D1127423

ALLEN COUNTY PUBLIC LIBRARY
FORT WAYNE, INDIANA 46802

SOARING

SOARING

Where Hawks and Eagles Fly

CHARLES COOMBS

Henry Holt and Company / New York

Allen County Public Library
Ft. Wayne, Indiana

To my brother,
Ronald "Brick" Coombs

Copyright © 1988 by Charles Coombs
All rights reserved, including the right to reproduce
this book or portions thereof in any form.
Published by Henry Holt and Company, Inc.,
115 West 18th Street, New York, New York 10011.
Published in Canada by Fitzhenry & Whiteside Limited,
195 Allstate Parkway, Markham, Ontario L3R 4T8.

Library of Congress Cataloging in Publication Data
Coombs, Charles Ira,
Soaring : where hawks and eagles fly.
Bibliography: p.
Includes index
Summary: Introduces the adventurous sport of
sailplaning and gliding by following a young
gliding enthusiast through the rigors of ground
school and flying lessons to his first solo flight
to a harrowing cross country flight.
1. Gliding and soaring—Juvenile literature.
[1. Gliding]   I. Title.
GV764.C66   1988   797.5'5   87-28370
ISBN 0-8050-0496-3

First Edition

Designer: Victoria Hartman
Printed in the United States of America
10 9 8 7 6 5 4 3 2 1

With the exception of those individually credited,
all photographs are by the author.

ISBN 0-8050-0496-3

Contents

Acknowledgments

I have been keenly interested in all aspects of aviation for as long as I can remember. Many of the greatest times of my life have been while flying in a large assortment of skycraft . . . from supersonic jets through helicopters to balloons. But somehow my experience with gliders had never gotten beyond writing a few magazine articles some years ago.

All that changed recently when I had the good fortune to meet a couple of devout glider pilots who willingly shared experiences with me. Both Chuck Stark and Jim Miller, members of the Cypress Soaring Club in Southern California, hold most of the awards you can earn in the world of soaring. I was in good hands, indeed.

But no matter what gliderport I visited, or what soaring enthusiasts I came in contact with, I found everyone helpful and full of good cheer. All were anxious to share the fun and excitement of their unique activity of sailing the skies on silent wings.

Beyond that, I received excellent cooperation from the Soaring Society of America, the nation's foremost authority on gliding activity. The SSA should be the first contact made by anyone seriously interested in taking up gliding.

Assorted sailplane manufacturers such as Schweizer Aircraft Corporation, Grob Systems, Inc., and Schempp-Hirth provided needed data and pictures. The U.S. Air Force Academy briefed me thoroughly on its use of sailplanes for cadet training and recreation.

To all those zestful people who made my book so exciting and interesting, many thanks.

Charles "Chick" Coombs
Westlake Village, California
1988

SOARING

The drifting object is a glider. *Schweizer Aircraft Corp.*

1

FLIGHT

*Y*ou see it circling in the distance, high in the sky. You brake your bike to a stop to get a better look. At first you think it's a hawk, or even an eagle. But it's way too big. And it's all white, except for what appears to be some kind of numbers or lettering on its tall tail. It keeps spiraling silently upward as though twirling on the end of an invisible string.

Curious, you take up the chase, pedaling hard, hoping to get a closer look. But it keeps climbing and getting farther away. It almost disappears into a woolly flat-bottomed cloud moving slowly across the sky.

Straining to keep your eyes on the flying object, you suddenly crash your bike into a curb, and tumble with a painful grunt into a patch of weeds beside the road. A dog barks wildly from behind a nearby chain-link fence. You untangle yourself from the bike and check your skinned elbow. You straighten up the handlebars, jump back onto the seat, and hurry on.

The drifting object is no longer up under the cloud. Slowly sinking, it weaves about the sky as though searching for something below. Its long white wings flash in the sun.

Now you are close enough to see it plainly. It's a *glider*. Sleek. Streamlined. No motor. No propeller. And it is obviously coming down.

There is no airport nearby, so whoever is flying the strange craft seems to be headed for a crash. You pedal furiously, trying to keep the descending aircraft in sight. Suddenly it drops from view beyond the high school buildings.

"Oh, no," your mind calls out. "Don't crash!"

Then, as you bank your bike around the corner of the gym, you sigh with relief. The aircraft is on the ground at the far end of the grassy football field. It's lopsided and resting on one wingtip, but doesn't seem to be damaged.

You pedal faster, and skid to a stop just as the clear Plexiglas bubble swings open over the pilot's head. A man pries himself up from the narrow opening, swings a leg over the edge of the enclosure, and steps out.

No, not a man . . . a boy . . . not much older than yourself. As you lay your bike on its side and hurry over, you notice he wears one of those white cloth tennis hats with the brim turned down all the way around. Sewn on it is a small emblem of a glider, and underneath are the words FALCON SOARING CLUB. He's dressed in plain jeans, a T-shirt, and scuffed tennis shoes.

"Hi," he says, smiling. "Seems I lost my *lift*."

"Lift?"

"Yeah. I was riding the warm air rising under that *cumulus* cloud." He points skyward. "It was a nice *thermal*. But its lift gave out suddenly. I had no choice but to come down. Tough. I was hoping to make it back to the *gliderport* at Hillcrest."

"Hillcrest? That's about ten miles from here. How could you reach Hillcrest without an engine?"

A glider has a single landing wheel; at rest it tilts onto one wingtip.

"*Glide*," the young pilot says. "In theory, this baby should glide about twenty-five feet forward for every foot of altitude it loses. From a mile high, under ideal conditions, I should be able to reach a landing spot twenty-five miles away. It's called the *glide ratio*, or lift over drag, *L/D* for short."

"Sounds complicated."

"Not really," he says. "Besides, all kinds of things upset the advertised glide ratio. When I ran out of thermal lift, I got caught in a headwind. My plans for getting back to Hillcrest went haywire. So I picked a landing spot."

"Wow. You took a big chance," you say. "What if the football field hadn't been here?"

"Oh, I had other, alternative landing places in view. This just looked like the best and the closest. But I had to watch out for the goalposts. I used my wing *spoilers* to slow down so I could come in over that fence and brake to a stop before running into those bleachers. No big deal. By the way, my name's Tom." He sticks out his hand.

You introduce yourself and ask, "What are you going to do now? Can you fly that thing out of here?"

"No way," he says, "but that's no problem. I've got a radio in the *cockpit*." He reaches under the tilted-up hood and lifts out a walkie-talkie radio. While flicking a switch, he raises the instrument to his mouth. "Oh-one-six to ground crew. I'm down safe on Fremont High School football field. Request *retrieve*. Over."

"Crew to oh-one-six," the reply comes quickly. "Roger. We were worried. Lost track of you. Should be there in about ten minutes."

Seeing the puzzled look on your face, the young flier explains. "That was my *crew*. Actually my older brother and his girlfriend, Shana. They're out there someplace with a trailer. They've been following and trying to keep me in sight. They did pretty well, if they're only ten minutes away."

Then he sits down in the cool shade of the glider's wing and invites you to join him. And, as you had hoped, he starts talking about gliding. By now several other curious young people have arrived. They start popping questions right and left.

In a matter-of-fact way Tom explains that just about everyone with normal health, average intelligence, decent eyesight—with or without glasses—determination, and good muscular coordination can learn to fly a glider. Age has little to do with it, although you must be fourteen to earn your student certificate and be allowed to fly alone, or *solo*. In fact, he says, lots of physically handicapped people who are unable to take part in other types of sporting activities make excellent glider pilots.

"Heck, we've got a member in our club who lost a leg in an

automobile accident. He rigged up a gadget to help him work the *rudder pedals*. He's one of our best pilots."

You listen closely as Tom goes on to describe how you earn a *student pilot* rating by studying and making a few flights with a qualified instructor.

"You start out," he says, "by learning about glider parts and how each functions. You learn the tricks of handling a glider on the ground. You master the important steps of *preflighting*, or carefully checking out a glider before a flight. You familiarize yourself with airport rules, various landing patterns, and the important *Federal Aviation Regulations (FARs)* that govern the flight of all aircraft. All in all, you learn the duties of a glider pilot."

He also mentions the importance of maintaining a *logbook*, a sort of diary that keeps track of your progress. All of this ground school teaching may take place before you even get a taste of flying, although chances are that along the way you will get a flight or two with a licensed pilot to help raise your interest.

"You can usually finish the ground school part in a few sessions," Tom says. "When your instructor is satisfied with what you have learned, he or she will issue you a valid *Federal Aviation Agency (FAA)* student glider pilot certificate. You are then ready to start your real flight training program."

Tom goes on to explain how the instructor takes you through advanced steps of learning what makes a glider fly. You become familiar with how various controls operate. Then, once in the air, you are ready to learn assorted maneuvers and emergency procedures.

"Finally," Tom concludes, "you take an oral exam on what you have learned, including the FARs. By that time you probably have made a dozen or so flights with your instructor. If you've paid attention, you should be ready for solo flight."

"Solo? All alone? That must be something."

"Believe me, it is. Just you and your glider and the big, big sky! There is nothing like it."

"Wow!"

Tom went on to explain that once you solo, you can work toward a *private pilot* license. For your private license you must be at least sixteen years old. Your carefully maintained logbook should show that you have made twenty or so flights, and have seven or more hours of solo time. You must also pass a written examination and be flight tested by someone approved by the FAA. From what Tom says, the FAA makes and enforces the rules that control all aspects of aviation in the United States. And that includes gliders, or *sailplanes*, as they are often called.

As a private pilot you are allowed to carry passengers if you like. But on pleasure trips only. You need a *commercial pilot* license to carry paying passengers. Many adventuresome people—young and old—enjoy the thrill of taking a glider flight with a properly skilled and licensed pilot. With a commercial license you may also become an FAA *Certified Flight Instructor (CFI)* with a glider rating. In gliding, a CFI, like the captain of a ship, is top rank.

You are really warming up to the subject of gliding, and bursting with more questions, when a van comes through an open gate and rolls lightly across the field. It is towing a long empty trailer behind it.

A young man with hair the same color as Tom's steps out of the van. He is followed by a freckle-nosed girl in faded blue jeans.

"Sorry, gang." Tom moves out from the shadow of the wing. "That's my crew. We've got to dismantle this bird, pack up, and head home."

A dismantled glider is transported on a specially fitted trailer.

You stand back and watch while the three take the glider apart and slide the assorted pieces into special racks built on the trailer.

When everything is packed and tied down, Tom comes over to you. "Thanks for the company," he says. "You really seem interested. You would probably make a good glider pilot. Think about it. Do some reading. Look through the issues of *Soaring* magazine at your library. It's published by the *Soaring Society of America*, or *SSA*, which is the big association for glider pilots in America. And there are books on gliding. Look under 'sailplaning' or 'soaring.' And, sometime when you come to Hillcrest, look me up. You can usually find me weekends at the gliderport just west of town."

With that, and a friendly wave to all who have gathered on the football field, pilot and crew leave, towing the trailer behind.

Deep in thought, you pedal over to the public library to do some browsing. Imagining yourself learning to fly like a bird, you go to the aviation section and explore the history of flight.

Leonardo da Vinci's birdlike ornithopter was a unique but unsuccessful idea for a man-powered flying machine. *IBM Corp.*

In the late fifteenth century, the Italian genius Leonardo da Vinci (1452–1519) invented, built, and tested air machines called *ornithopters* that tried to copy the flight of birds. Leonardo's idea was sound enough. However, man simply did not have the muscle power to flap the wings vigorously enough to lift the heavy ornithopters off the ground.

Eighteenth-century ballooning gave people the feeling of flying. But the gas-filled or hot-air balloons went only where the breezes took them. They simply did not provide the type of controlled flight that people were seeking.

Late in the nineteenth century, in Germany, Otto Lilienthal (1848–1896) made several wood-and-fabric gliders. To make these gliders "fly," Lilienthal would make a running start down a high knoll, launch himself into the wind, tuck in his feet, and sail through the air before coming back to earth. During an early flight he sailed some hundred and fifty feet, and within a few weeks Lilienthal was making gliding flights of a quarter-mile or so. But such gliding could not truly be called flying. Lilienthal had very little control over the aircraft, and could only glide downward from some high spot of ground.

Meanwhile, in America, Wilbur (1867–1912) and Orville (1871–1948) Wright virtually abandoned their successful bicycle business in Dayton, Ohio, to continue experimenting with Lilienthal's theories of manned flight. They added many of their own ideas. They also received advice from Octave Chanute, a fellow American who had done much study and experimental work in the field of flying, or *aeronautics*.

Needing a reliable source of wind and some fairly high ground from which to launch their home-built gliders, the Wright brothers moved to the seaside sand dunes near Kitty Hawk, North Carolina. The Wright brothers' early efforts included many failures. During the year 1902, however, from the sand dunes of Kill Devil Hill, not far down the beach from Kitty Hawk, Wilbur and Orville made hundreds of short flights gliding into the wind. That year they also made a major breakthrough: By attaching control wires to the wingtips in such a way that they could use them to twist or warp the wings, Wilbur and Orville devised a way to turn the glider. Occasionally they were even able to gain a little altitude during a flight . . . to truly *soar*, rather than simply glide downward in the wind.

What they learned through these flights spurred the Wright brothers to build a motor-powered glider. On December 17, 1903, from the same sand dunes near Kitty Hawk, they made the world's first propeller-driven aircraft flights . . . bringing about the modern age of aviation.

The age of American aviation began when the Wright brothers added an engine and propellers to a basic glider, and flew from Kitty Hawk. *Smithsonian Institution*

Although engine-powered flight slowed down interest in gliding, it didn't end it. Many adventuresome young crafts-men continued to build and fly wood-ribbed, cloth-covered, primitive primary gliders of their own designs.

Meanwhile, in 1918 World War I ended. Part of the Treaty of Versailles prohibited vanquished nations from building and flying motorized aircraft for fear that they could be turned into war machines. However, gliders were allowed. Indeed, the resourceful Germans built and flew them by the thousands. They developed light, long-winged gliders that could soar upward on gently rising air currents. Called sailplanes, after their ability to cruise through the air, they were the first true soaring aircraft. By the outbreak of World War II, the Germans had trained nearly 200,000 youths to fly gliders. With a little extra instruction, they later became the fighter and bomber pilots who made up the German air force, or *Luftwaffe*. Similar inexpensive gliders were manufactured and used for training pilots in England, America, and other countries being drawn into the conflict.

After the war there was a ready market for the sleek train-

Sailplaning is part of the flight training program at the U.S. Air Force Academy. *U.S. Air Force Academy*

ing sailplanes that had suddenly become items of war surplus. People got together and formed gliding clubs. They pooled their dues to purchase and learn to fly the motorless aircraft. The U.S. Air Force Academy, nestled in the Colorado Rocky Mountains, adopted the use of gliders in its flight training program. Factories in America and abroad began building sailplanes in order to fill the growing demand. Soaring, as you might say, was suddenly on the rise.

By the time you leave the library and start pedaling homeward, you want to take part in the art, sport, and challenge of learning to fly on wings in the wind.

$$\sim\!\!2$$

THE GLIDERS

*O*n your next free Saturday, after you finish doing a
few chores around the house, you hop on your
bike and pedal to Hillcrest.

The gliderport is about two miles west of town. The two-
lane road leading out to it winds through the wooded
foothills, then flattens and follows the floor of a broad valley.
At a signpost with a missing L that reads SAILP ANE ENTER-
PRISES, you turn off onto a gravel road and ride until you
reach a mobile trailer unit that serves as a flight operations
shack.

Beyond the shack, a collection of gliders catches your eye.
As you walk among them, you notice names such as
Schweizer, Glaser-Dirks, Grob, Pik, Schleicher, Blanik,
Schempp-Hirth, and Glasfugel stenciled on their sides. Soaring is a worldwide activity. A few of the gliders have unique
designs and simple names. You imagine some are homebuilts, perhaps put together from plans or kits in someone's
garage or shop.

You notice one long-winged sailplane that has a small
motor and propeller mounted above the body, or *fuselage*.
From your library research you recognize it to be a

A sign with a missing letter L leads to the gliderport.

motorglider. The self-propelled craft can take off on its own power, climb to altitude, then have the engine shut off and become a true sailplane. Painted on each aircraft are large serial numbers. Most are preceded by the letter N, indicating that it is registered in the United States. A few carry letters of registry from other countries.

It is now nearly noon, and the gliderport has come alive. While some people start moving their gliders toward the airstrip, others are busy assembling aircraft from assorted parts they pull out of a variety of long, covered cocoonlike trailers. Still others arrive on open trailers like the one used that day on the football field.

The sailplanes come in an assortment of sizes and colors, although most are white. They all sit low to the ground, usually supported by a single main wheel that is recessed

A collection of gliders.

into the underside of the fuselage. Some have skids; others have small wheels near the front and rear to protect the nose or tail from scraping the ground. The wingtips are also protected by some kind of roller or skid.

Suddenly you hear the roar of an airplane taking off. You glance toward the field just in time to see a small single-engine plane towing a sleek glider to the air at the end of a long yellow rope. At the far end of the paved airstrip several other sailplanes have lined up awaiting their turn for a tow. About a hundred yards beyond them still more sailplanes have gathered at the end of what appears to be a dirt strip. You are trying to figure out why they would be over there when you hear a voice at your side.

"Hi." You turn to see Tom smiling at you. "I'm glad you decided to come out here and see what it's all about."

"You invited me. Remember?"

"You bet. And I've got a little time before I have to line up for an *aero tow*. Come on. I'll show you around."

He quickly explains that the gliders you have just noticed off beyond the main airstrip are waiting their turns for a *winch* tow. For the first time you see the heavy piece of machinery standing at the far end of a long, well-worn dirt strip. It looks like a large spool mounted on an old truck chassis.

"It's a cable winch," Tom explains. "It can't launch you as high, nor drop you in a thermal area like a *towplane*, or *tug*, can. But it comes in handy on a busy day like this when you may have to wait an hour or more for a turn at the towplane. And it's a lot quicker and less expensive than an aero tow, which may cost from ten to twenty dollars." Tom also mentions that it was once a common practice to tow a glider into the air behind an automobile.

"Neither winch nor auto tows are used much these days," he says. "Aero tows are gentler on a glider, and, well, better all around." He glances at his wristwatch. "Hey, it's later than I thought. I'm afraid I'll have to get ready for my flight. Maybe later . . . but wait, here comes Shana. She got her private license about a week ago. And she knows her sailplanes."

Tom leaves, and Shana takes over. While walking toward the flight line, she tells you how much she enjoys serving on a glider crew when she's not flying.

"As a crew member," she says, "you learn about gliders firsthand. Tracking a glider from the ground gives you experience with air-to-ground communication, map reading, and navigation. You learn about the weather conditions that provide lift to keep the glider up, or generate *sink* that brings it down. You learn to assemble a glider, or to dismantle, or *derig*, it after a flight and pack it away. And, most of the time, crewing is just plain fun."

You make a mental note that, in case you take up gliding, you will volunteer for work on a crew in order to gain important experience.

Shana pauses at a group of parked planes. She explains that gliders and sailplanes are considered the same. However, in the old sense of the word, a glider flies a downward path, constantly losing altitude, while a lightweight sailplane with its long wing is able to soar upward on currents of rising air. Still, the government officially refers to all such aircraft as gliders. So, in fact, do most soaring enthusiasts. Glider is a simple, convenient word.

In starting to describe a glider, Shana breaks it down into three main parts—fuselage, wing, and tail.

The fuselage is the body of the glider. The wing and tail are attached to it. The fuselage also has room for a cockpit where the pilot and perhaps a passenger ride.

The wing furnishes the lift that makes the aircraft fly. Located along the *trailing edge* of the wing and just inward from each wingtip is an *aileron*. The aileron is a narrow, hinged, oblong panel. Its movement is controlled from the cockpit. When the aileron on one wing tilts up, the one on the opposite wing tilts down. This deflects the airstream unevenly and causes the glider to tip or roll sideways. The wing also contains the spoilers that thrust out into the airstream to disrupt or "spoil" part of the wing's lift. This slows the aircraft and causes it to lose altitude, which may be particularly useful during a landing. Some glider wings may have moving *flaps* along their trailing edge. When partially extended, flaps provide extra surface and add more lift to the wing. Fully extended, however, they dip down into the airstream and act as brakes or spoilers to slow the aircraft down.

The tail, or *empennage*, is made up of a horizontal *stabilizer* and a vertical *fin*. The stabilizer acts like a small wing to keep the glider's tail up and flying level. A hinged vane, or *elevator*, that stretches along the trailing edge of the stabilizer is

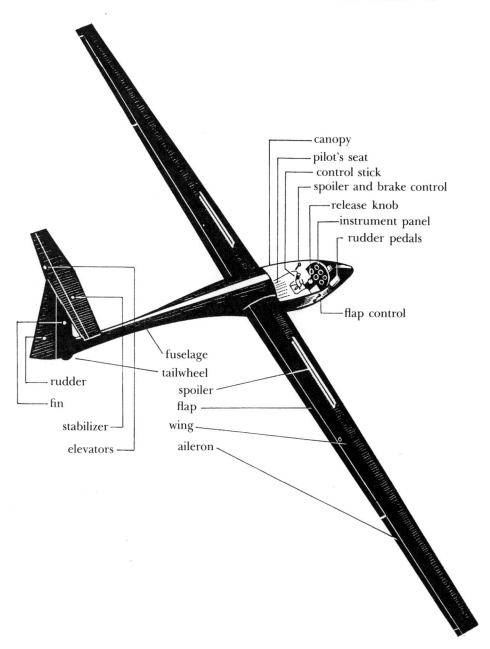

canopy
pilot's seat
control stick
spoiler and brake control
release knob
instrument panel
rudder pedals

flap control

fuselage
tailwheel
rudder
spoiler
fin
flap
stabilizer
wing
elevators
aileron

The parts of a sailplane. *Soaring Society of America*

used to move the glider's tail up or down, causing the plane to dive or climb. The solid upright fin, sometimes called the *vertical stabilizer*, helps keep the sailplane flying a straight course. Attached to the fin's trailing edge is a movable *rudder* that is used to change direction, much like the rudder on a boat.

These are the glider's main parts and control surfaces. The controls are moved by wires or jointed rods that are operated from inside the cockpit by a *control stick*, a pair of *rudder pedals*, and an assortment of handles and knobs.

Some gliders are built around a wood or metal framework and covered with tightly stretched fabric or a metal skin such as a lightweight aluminum. However, many of the modern, high-performance sailplanes are formed by bonding and shaping layers of fiberglass or carbon fiber compounds. Such high-tech materials are strong, durable, lightweight, and easy to maintain.

Since gliders have no engines and few moving parts, and undergo much less stress and vibration than motorized aircraft, they usually last much longer. Some gliders, Shana tells you, are twenty or thirty years old and still in good flying condition.

The various instruments that tell the pilot what is happening during a flight are located in the glider's cockpit. Shana goes on to describe the gadgets and dials displayed on the front panel. Each is designed to record some element of the flight.

"Your senses can deceive you when you are high in the sky," she explains. "It is hard to judge speed, height, distance, or really what you are doing without the help of instruments."

The most important instruments in a glider are the *altimeter*, *airspeed indicator* (*ASI*), *variometer*, and *compass*.

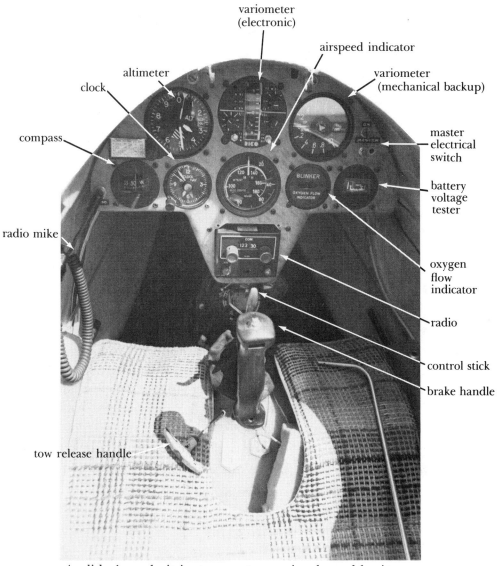

variometer
(electronic)

airspeed indicator

variometer
(mechanical backup)

altimeter

clock

master
electrical
switch

compass

battery
voltage
tester

radio mike

oxygen
flow
indicator

radio

control stick

brake handle

tow release handle

A glider's cockpit instruments are simple and basic.

The altimeter tells you in hundreds and thousands of feet just how high you are above ground level (AGL), or above mean sea level (MSL), depending upon how you set the instrument. The airspeed indicator does exactly what its name implies. It tells how fast you are going through the air. A red mark on its face warns you to keep below the *red line* speed for safety. An aircraft is not designed to go beyond the red line speed, which varies with each make of aircraft.

The variometer, which most glider pilots simply call a *vario*, indicates the sailplane's rate of climb, which is called lift, or its rate of descent, which is called *sink*. On most varios a needle swings up or down on a scale, telling you whether your aircraft is being lifted by air currents, or is sinking in a downdraft.

In flight, a quick glance at the variometer tells you in hundreds of feet per minute just how fast the air around you is moving up or down. Although your glider won't be able to match the speed of the upward movement of the air, due to weight and air friction, the vario gives an indication of the strength of lift that you may expect. Most varios have a backup audio tone built into them, so you won't need to keep your eyes riveted on the needle. The greater the lift and the faster the climb, the more strident the tone becomes. A glider pilot learns to judge by the volume and pitch of the hum or squeal just about how fast he or she is climbing without even looking at the vario. Varios are so important to soaring that many sailplanes carry a second or backup vario in case one should malfunction.

The compass is needed to keep you on course during long *cross-country* flights.

Some sailplanes also carry a *turn and bank indicator* to let you know whether you are flying your glider with smooth, well-coordinated movements of the controls, or whether you are slipping and sliding haphazardly through the sky.

"Actually," Shana tells you, "the fewer instruments you have to look at, the easier it is to keep your gaze outside of the cockpit. You need to keep looking around outside, clearing the sky to be sure you don't tangle with another aircraft. And being able to enjoy the scenery is one of the best parts of sailplaning."

Then, kind of as a final note, she points to a short eight-inch piece of orange yarn, with one end taped to the outside front of the transparent cockpit enclosure.

Shana anticipates your question. "That's called a *yaw string*. It's the best turn and bank indicator around. It's the cheapest part of the glider. Costs maybe a penny. But it's one of the most important instruments we have."

Then, before she can explain further, you hear footsteps at your side. You turn to see a vaguely familiar face. Then you recognize it as belonging to Tom's older brother, who had come to pick him up at the football field that day.

"I'm glad to see you out here," he says. "I kind of had you figured as a guy who would be interested in this sort of thing. You have that look of adventure in your eyes."

You like that, even though it makes you blush a bit.

Then he springs a surprise. "How would you like to go for a little glider ride?"

Before you can answer, he explains that he wants to check out the wing spoilers of the club's two-seater airplane. The mechanic has done some work on them, and he wants to try them out on a short flight, using the winch tow.

"You mean take a test flight?" you ask eagerly.

"Well, not just like you've seen in the movies," he says, smiling. "But maybe . . ."

"Wow."

Since you are still a minor, he says that you need a signed release before he can take you up. "Maybe you better call your parents first," he suggests. "If they approve, I'll run you into Fremont to get the release signed."

A few minutes later, your mother sounds a bit hesitant,

but summons your father to the phone. He asks a few questions, then talks a minute to the pilot. Then he gets you back on the line. "Bring the release," he says. You can almost sense a note of envy in his voice.

Later, you help push the two-seater over to the site where the winch is operating. You can barely control your excitement as the veteran pilot directs you to climb into the front seat. He helps you fasten the seat belt and shoulder harness. He cautions you to keep your hands and feet clear of the control stick and rudder pedals, as he will use the dual set of controls in the back seat to fly the plane. But you have no intention to push, pull, twist, or do anything with the assorted knobs, switches, handles, and levers that surround you. Since the glider tilts toward one wingtip resting on the ground, you sit a bit lopsided in the shallow bucket seat.

After checking the aircraft over carefully, the pilot climbs into the seat directly behind you. The foot pedals and the stick between your knees move as he tests the controls from the rear seat.

Meanwhile, outside the cockpit Shana leans down and snaps the ring spliced to the end of the long thin towing cable to the hook under the glider's nose. You notice a small parachute attached to the cable a few feet out from the end. At the far end of the dirt strip, you can barely make out the winch operator waiting for the signal to start reeling in the cable.

After testing the hook and cable connection, Shana moves out and lifts the low wingtip so the glider sits level. Beyond her a flagman waits to signal the distant winch operator when the pilot is ready. After one more check of the controls, the pilot pulls the clear plastic canopy down over your heads and locks it.

"Ready?" he asks behind you.

A glider receiving a winch tow with a vintage drum-and-cable system.

"Roger!" you reply . . . straight out of a TV flying adventure.

You can't see the pilot signal his readiness, but suddenly the flagman waves his banner. The cable pulls taut. The glider surges forward, quickly picking up speed. Shana runs along for a few steps holding up the wingtip. But as soon as the speed is sufficient for the controls to take over, she lets go.

The increasing acceleration thrusts you back against the seat. The scenery rushes past in a blur. You feel the jarring of the landing wheel as it bounces off the uneven ground beneath you. The glider's aluminum skin snaps and crackles with each small bump.

Then the stick comes back and the plane's nose pitches up steeply. You stare up into an empty sky as the glider accelerates during the climb. You feel the vibrating strain of the sharply tilted wing against the forward pull of the thin cable.

The sailplane climbs steeply before releasing the winch cable.

You wonder how long the pilot can keep the aircraft in such a steep climb before the winch starts tugging it back down toward the ground. You thrill at the unique sensation of gravity forcing you against the back rest.

Then suddenly the glider noses down, and you hear the clack of the hook opening. You can't see the cable drop away, but you can visualize its loose end falling gently back to the ground under the small parachute.

The pull of gravity eases off, replaced by the delightful feel of floating freely. The pilot steers the glider into a gentle turn. You look down toward the airfield, fascinated by the sight of the toylike winch at one end and the cluster of birdlike gliders waiting their turns at the other end. You gaze all around, glorying at the sight of a strange new world stretching out below.

"How do you like it?" Although he speaks in normal tones, the pilot's voice is plainly heard over the soft hissing of the airstream brushing against the outside of the airplane. He banks the glider on its side to give you a still better look at the multicolored landscape. Your eyes can't seem to take in enough. Your mind revels in the thrill of your new discovery—flight.

"Great!" It's the only word that comes to mind.

He cruises around for a few minutes. Occasionally you hear a gentle hum from the variometer. You glance at the needle to see it tilted slightly above horizontal, indicating pockets of weak lift. Often, however, the needle dips downward, indicating sink. But the pilot had said it would be a short flight. As you glide back toward the gliderport, he tells

A gliderport.

Coming in with spoilers open.

you to look out at the wing. As you do, you see the long narrow spoilers slide up and down in the recessed wing slots as he works the lever from the rear cockpit. Each time the spoilers poke up into the airstream, the aircraft shudders slightly, slows down, and drops its nose.

"They test out fine," the pilot says. "We better go back in. There's not much lift around here."

He circles the field in a sloping glide, then lines the glider's nose up with the landing strip. When the plane gets lower you feel the increasing speed as it streaks over the ground. The stick then comes back. You brace yourself as the glider levels off, settles the final few feet, and touches down with scarcely a jar.

It coasts about a hundred feet before the pilot applies the

brake. The glider rolls to a stop, and tilts leisurely over onto one wingtip.

You sit still for a moment, taking in the experience of your first glider flight. As you start unbuckling your seat belt and shoulder harness, one thought is uppermost in your mind. If there is anything you can do about it, this will not be your last glider flight.

3

WHY THEY FLY

*A*fter thanking his older brother for the flight, you go looking for Tom. You catch up with him just as he is pushing a sleek fiberglass single-seater off the runway, where another Falcon Soaring Club member is waiting to take it up.

"Did you have a good flight?" you ask Tom.

"Pretty good," he says, wiping sweat from his face. "But it was short . . . and hot in the cockpit. I couldn't find enough lift to get me up where the cold air is. Let's go get a Coke."

There's a shaded picnic table near the vending machine. You sit and visit. Tom advises you to talk to your parents about wanting to fly gliders. He suggests, however, that you learn as much as you can about flying in general before you go to them.

"If you know what you're talking about," he says, "they will figure that you're serious."

So you start by sitting in on a couple of free discussion sessions the club sets up to introduce sailplaning to anybody who is interested. You learn that Hillcrest is just one of some eighty or so certified glider flying schools in the United States. And, in addition to the Falcon Soaring Club, close to three hundred other similar sailplaning clubs, large and small, are scattered throughout most of the states. Canada, Australia, Europe, and Asia have widespread sailplaning activities. In the United States you need only inquire at a local airport or send a query to the SSA in order to locate a soaring facility reasonably nearby.

It is important to get some ground school training before you attempt to pilot a glider. Unless you are a somewhat slow learner, three or four sessions of ground school should get you ready for the cockpit, where you can put your knowledge to work in the air.

The Falcons, you are delighted to learn, don't charge dues-paying junior members for ground school. There will be enough other costs later on. Having some information at hand, you present your case at home. Your folks listen, ask a few questions, and, after a bit of discussion, give their OK. That is, they won't issue a protest as long as learning to soar doesn't interfere with your schoolwork and other duties.

You know you are going to need money for club dues, gliding lessons, towing fees, and all that. You can't see how you can get along on less than thirty or forty dollars a month. Even though you've heard that the club makes it as easy as possible on its junior members, it will probably cost you three hundred to four hundred dollars by the time you have learned enough to solo. And, although your paper route earnings will almost cover it, it's still big money. But, with a little coaxing, your dad agrees to help take up the slack, provided you are willing to take on a couple of extra chores around the house.

The next weekend you sign up for ground school. At the first session the instructor starts with a warning to the seven in your class. "Just remember, you take a risk whenever you leave the ground," he says. "Height isn't important. Whether you fall a hundred feet or five thousand feet, the results are fairly similar and can be disastrous. So, for safety and enjoyment, prepare yourselves thoroughly before attempting to take any flying machine off the ground."

He contends that learning what makes a sailplane fly is the best place to start. He calls it *aerodynamics*. And just so you won't forget, he writes it on the chalkboard: AERO-DYNAMICS—THE SCIENCE OF FLIGHT WITHIN THE EARTH'S ATMOSPHERE.

Aerodynamics, as he explains it, deals with four major forces that affect the flight of an aircraft. They are *lift*, *gravity* (or weight), *thrust*, and *drag*.

Lift is generated when a fast-moving stream of air passes over and under the aircraft's specially shaped wing, also called an airfoil. The wing has a little more curve on the top than on the bottom. When the plane moves forward at a fast enough speed, pressure increases on the underside of the wing, but decreases to sort of a vacuum over the curved top. With positive pressure pushing from below and negative pressure, or a vacuum, offering no resistance from above,

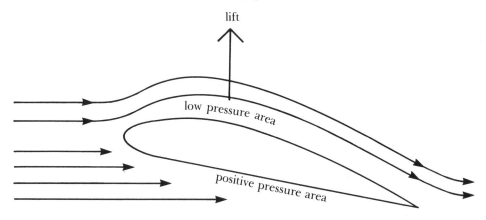

Wing shape and airspeed help produce lift. *U.S. Dept. of Transportation*

the wing rises upward, taking plane and pilot with it.

In order to produce the proper amount of lift, the wing should tilt up slightly into the airstream. This upward tilt is called the *angle of attack*. Some angle of attack is designed

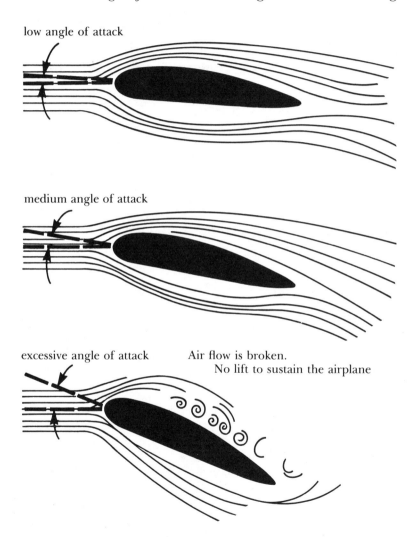

low angle of attack

medium angle of attack

excessive angle of attack   Air flow is broken.
No lift to sustain the airplane

Angle of attack may increase lift or produce a dangerous stall. *U.S. Dept. of Transportation*

into the aircraft. But the angle of attack is also increased or decreased by raising or lowering the glider's nose during flight.

Up to a point, the greater the angle of attack, the more lift. You can see how this works by sticking your hand out the window of a moving car. If you hold your hand parallel to the ground, nothing really happens. But if you tilt your hand up or down, you feel the airstream force it up or down. You have simply changed the angle of attack, the same as you would with an aircraft's wing.

But the angle of attack must be controlled. If you tilt the wing too steeply, burbles of air form on top of it and destroy the lift. Unless you drop the nose and decrease the angle of attack, the glider will lose its essential flying speed and stop, or *stall*, in midair.

Maintaining proper lift is important, but it's not the whole story. Two other forces constantly stage a tug-of-war to determine whether the aircraft will keep moving or fall back to earth. These opposing forces are thrust and drag. While thrust moves an aircraft forward, drag tries to hold it back. Drag is primarily the friction of air brushing against the wings, fuselage, and tail. Drag works upon everything that moves on land, through the sea, or in the air. It is the enemy of thrust. And thrust is what moves an aircraft.

But, wait, aircraft thrust usually depends upon engines, propellers, jets, or rockets. A glider doesn't have any of these thrust-producing devices to propel it forward. So how do you get a glider to keep flying once it is released from tow and is on its own?

Quite simply, a sailplane produces its own forward momentum by using gravity. Gravity tries to pull a sailplane straight back to earth, just as it tries to pull any object back to earth. Supported by its broad high-lift wing, the sailplane noses down, allowing gravity to pull it, thus gaining forward speed. In order to keep going, it must keep gliding downward. Its speed depends largely upon the steepness or shallowness of the glide. In any case, much of gravity's downward pull is converted to a descending forward motion. This can be called the glider's thrust.

"So gravity plays a dual role," your instructor says. "It opposes the lift that you need to stay aloft. But it also pulls the glider forward. And pull is certainly a form of thrust. You deal with the four forces I've mentioned by carefully controlling your aircraft."

You remember how Shana had described briefly the various control surfaces on the aircraft, and the stick, pedals, knobs, and handles that operate them. Now your instructor further emphasizes their importance. He explains how an aircraft responds to the movement of the controls by rotating in any of three directions on any of three *axes*. An axis is simply an imaginary or theoretical line drawn through the aircraft. The *longitudinal*, or long, *axis* stretches through the length of the glider, from nose to tail. The *lateral*, or wide, *axis* extends from wingtip to wingtip. The *vertical*, or up-and-down, *axis* sticks straight up through the middle point of the glider. That middle point is called the *center of gravity*, or *CG*. This is the spot where all three of the axes come together. It is the focal point on which the aircraft would balance if it were dangled from a string.

Any movement made by the aircraft disturbs its center of gravity. Each maneuver causes the glider to rotate around any or all of its three axes. By pushing or pulling the control stick forward or back, you make it *pitch* down or up, or around its lateral axis. Push the stick to one side and you make the plane *roll* around the longitudinal axis. Press one or the other rudder pedal and the aircraft's nose will waggle,

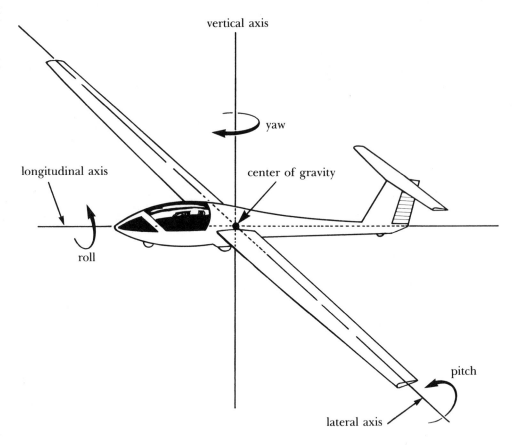

The aircraft moves or rotates around any or all of three axes.
Soaring Society of America

or *yaw*, from side to side around the vertical axis. Pitch, roll, and yaw—those are the three movements that can be made around the three axes.

In time, the instructor promises, you will learn to maneuver the glider by using carefully coordinated movements of the stick and rudder pedals. You will almost unconsciously combine elements of pitch, roll, and yaw to produce a smooth climbing turn, perhaps a quick change of direction to dodge around a rain squall, or to sideslip the glider onto the field during a crosswind landing.

"I've probably used some big words," he says, smiling.

lift

drag

thrust

gravity (weight)

With proper control of the four forces of lift, gravity, thrust, and drag, a sailplane flies smoothly. *Schweizer Aircraft Corp.*

"Don't let it worry you. Flying a glider is not as complicated as it may sound. With a little practice, it all becomes second nature."

You hope he's right!

4

SENSE OF THE SKY

*B*efore he is willing to let you go on to flying lessons, your ground school instructor insists that you know something about what to look for once you get up in the air. Since a glider is a heavier-than-air machine, once it has been cut loose from its tow vehicle, gravity will pull it quickly back to earth unless you can figure out some way to make it stay up. This means that you need some kind of fuel, some source of propulsion, if you hope to stay up for an extended length of time.

The source of propulsion that the instructor talks about is lift. You can't usually see, hear, touch, taste, or smell it. But lift is frequently somewhere around you . . . if you can just find it.

Air is not a placid, transparent void of nothingness. The air, or atmosphere, has substance to it. It is a constantly moving, churning, swirling mass of thin atom-filled matter. It's the movement of this air that provides the fuel for your motorless glider.

Generally speaking, glider lift is the product of air that is moving upward. If the force of the upward movement equals or exceeds the combined weight of the aircraft and pilot, the glider will stay up. If not, or if the air moves downward, the glider sinks. A glider pilot's main function is to seek lift and avoid sink.

The subject of lift versus sink comes under the general heading of *meteorology*, the science of weather and how it acts. Meteorology constantly affects your life. It helps you decide whether to wear a T-shirt or a wool sweater to school. It lets you know when to put away your skateboard and start waxing your skis. It tells you when it's safe to fly, or warns you when to stay on the ground.

The one sure thing about the weather is that it is always on the move. Even when you think it is dead calm, the air circulates gently around you. It can speed up to generate a kite-flying breeze, or it can become a raging, tree-toppling storm. It can be clear and bright, socked in with fog, or roofed over by clouds.

Like gravity, weather can be both a valued friend and a dangerous enemy to a sailplane pilot. So you spend time learning about the winds and the clouds that often accompany them. You learn to read the signs that indicate a change in weather. High clouds seldom drop rain; low clouds often do. Steeply rising smoke foretells fair weather. When smoke hugs the ground, it usually indicates lowering atmospheric pressure and a chance of rain. There are many ways of predicting weather, each with varying degrees of reliability.

You learn how weather changes can work both for and against your sailplaning adventures. Low pressure that brings rain usually brings poor flying conditions for a glider pilot. But a moving cold front that pushes in under a layer of warm air can provide fine lift for a sailplane.

Various types of clouds are usually dependable indicators of weather conditions. They are the signposts of the sky in

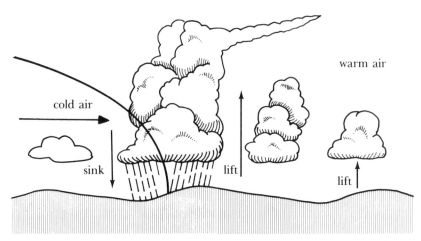

cold air

warm air

sink

lift

lift

The collision of cold and warm air masses generates weather changes that affect the glider pilot. *U.S. Dept. of Transportation*

which you will be flying. Usually low layers or sheets of clouds, known as *stratus*, indicate smooth air near the ground. But this will not be to your liking, for a glider flight relies on air that is not smooth. Gliders need air that is in motion, or unstable. Ground-heated air that moves vigorously upward from warm surfaces of the earth to form upwelling thermals is the most desirable.

Your instructor goes on then to describe three major types of air currents that you, as a glider pilot, can make use of. They are *ridge winds*, atmospheric *lee waves*, and, of course, *thermals*.

Ridge lift occurs when a stiff breeze of, say, ten to twenty miles an hour blows squarely up a hillside and on over its crest. The momentum of the wind glancing upward off the slope provides the glider pilot with a ride on the band or ribbon of upwelling air just above the ridge. Probably the most famous ridgeline in America stretches along the Allegheny Mountains, reaching all the way from Pennsylvania to Georgia. Sailplanes have soared back and forth along that ridge of hills on flights of more than a thousand nonstop miles.

The same type of ridge soaring is possible when a sea breeze glances upward off an oceanside cliff, or palisade, providing a similar band of rising air along its upper edge. Ridge riding, of course, is totally dependent upon a steady wind blowing at almost a right angle to the upthrusting land.

In ridge soaring, you must stay slightly on the windward or upwind side of the high ground in order to ride the band of rising air. If you drift downwind of the ridge, to the lee side, you are apt to get caught in an area of dangerous sink caused by the wind curling over and down the far side.

Though usually confined to flying at low altitude and lim-

Ridge lift along an ocean palisade enables a glider to cruise back and forth as long as the breeze keeps up.

ited to the length of the ridge or palisade, ridge running is a popular form of sailplaning. Ridge runners can stay aloft, shuttling back and forth along the range of hills just as long as the breeze holds. Sometimes a breeze will continue for several days and nights. In fact, years ago the practice of setting time-endurance records for gliders was abandoned. It was just too dangerous. Pilots were likely to succumb to exhaustion and fall asleep at the controls.

The practice of wave soaring is less common than sail-planing along ridges. It is also more complicated. To understand what a mountain *lee wave* is, visualize a large rock or water-soaked log barely submerged below the surface of a fast-moving stream. Notice how the water forms an initial bulge, or wave, at the obstruction. Then the water sinks into a hollow just downstream of the submerged object, and rises again into a second but smaller wave. The process continues with each ripple decreasing in size until the water flattens out again.

Wind often acts the same way, forming a series of waves and hollows downwind from, or on the lee side of, a range of hills or mountains. Lee waves that form beyond the eastern slopes of the Sierra Nevada Mountains in California can carry a sailplane to astounding altitudes of around fifty thousand feet . . . well into the area where extra oxygen and pressurization are needed for survival.

Indeed, wave soaring tests the mettle of any glider pilot. Even if you become skilled at it, you must take extreme care not to get trapped in a *rotor*, the churning whirlpool of air that usually circulates beneath a lee wave. A rotor is capable of tearing a glider apart, or hurtling it earthward.

You decide then and there that, exciting and challenging though it sounds, you will hold off on wave soaring until you become an expert sailplane pilot. Much more to your liking

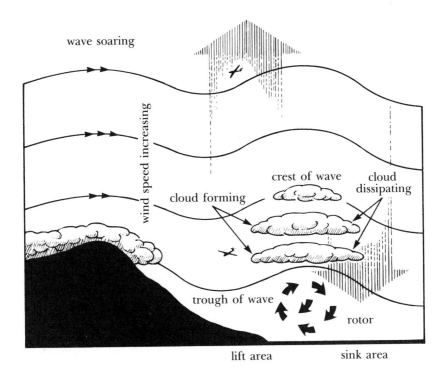

wave soaring

wind speed increasing

crest of wave

cloud dissipating

cloud forming

trough of wave

rotor

lift area

sink area

Wave soaring is the ultimate in sailplaning. *Soaring Society of America*

is the instructor's description of thermals. They are the main fuel used in modern soaring.

Thermaling is simply riding upward on a current of rising air. A thermal gets its warmth from the sun heating the ground. The sun's intense rays are readily absorbed by dark objects such as a freshly plowed field or the asphalt surface of a parking lot. As surface temperature increases, much of the heat is transferred to the air just above. The warming air expands and becomes lighter than the more dense cool air surrounding it. Thus a large bubble of warm air forms above the heated surface.

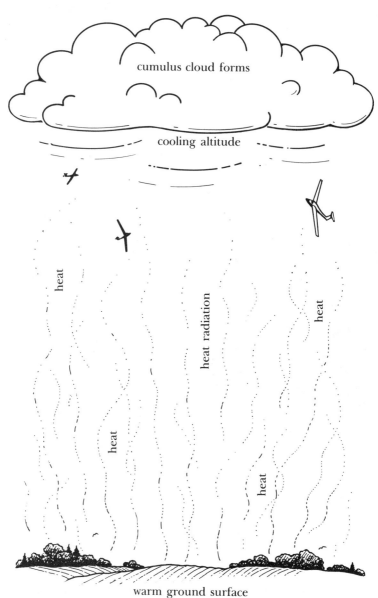

A thermal.

When the bubble grows big and buoyant enough, it breaks away from the surface. It starts to rise like a giant hot-air balloon. As it rises, more cool air flows in to fill the space just vacated. That air, too, heats up, breaks away, and follows the other bubble skyward. The process keeps repeating itself. These bubbles of warm air . . . one atop the other . . . form a veritable column of rising air—a thermal.

The temperature of the atmosphere decreases at the rate of 5½ degrees Fahrenheit for each thousand-foot increase in altitude. Thus, as the thermal rises in the sky, it cools. At an altitude where the temperature becomes cold enough to condense the molecules of water vapor within the thermal, a cloud forms. You've noticed how your warm breath forms a cloud of vapor in the icy air of a winter day. It's the same principle at work.

The fluffy white cloud that grows atop a thermal is called a *cumulus*, or *cu* for short. Cumulus clouds are the major road signs marking the location of thermals that produce lift for the glider. When cu's remain white and puffy and move slowly across the sky, they form a *cloud street*. If you are lucky enough to be in the air when a cloud street forms, you can hop from cloud to cloud on a long cross-country flight. This is thermaling at its very best.

However, at a higher altitude the cumulus may thicken and turn ragged. Or it may break up into *altocumulus* cotton-balls that cover the sky and usually signal a change in weather . . . a time for caution. Whenever clouds begin to stack up and form towering, churning gray and white masses known as *cumulonimbus*, meaning "piled-up rain cloud," the red warning flag is out. Stay clear! Inside of the bulbous mass is a world of cyclonic winds that throw fist-sized hailstones through jumbled streaks of lightning. This is nature on a rampage. Such thunderheads can suck in and destroy a glider.

Since thermals depend upon solar heating of large surfaces that absorb heat and transfer the warmth to the air above them, thermaling is primarily a warm-weather activity. Generally the spring and summer seasons produce the best soaring weather. And the best time is usually midday or

Cumulonimbus, or thunderheads, are avoided by all sensible glider pilots.

early afternoon, when the overhead sun directs its strongest rays to the ground.

But different surfaces generate different amounts of heat. An industrial area, a rock mesa, or a sun-drenched sandy beach often give birth to good thermals. Green fields, woodlands, wet ground, or lakes are apt to produce just the opposite, down currents of sinking air. A thermal might be no bigger than the dust devil you often see swirling over some field. But it could be a mile across, if the surface from which it radiates is also a mile across. Most thermals fit within a diameter of a couple hundred yards.

Not all thermals are marked by cumulus cloud tops. When there is an absence of moisture in the atmosphere, dry thermals are likely to form. They are called "blue thermals," since they may occur in cloudless blue skies. They are just as buoyant as any other thermal, but more difficult to locate in the absence of the fluffy signpost of a cu.

All in all, you soon become increasingly aware that the very essence of soaring is working with nature. You will use what nature offers by way of lift. You will heed its warnings. You will avoid the causes of sink. You will fly in harmony with what the sky has to offer.

It takes a couple weekends for you to complete your ground school courses and pass an oral test. You devote considerable time to helping around the gliderport. You help pilots make their preflight checks. You learn to hook up the tow ropes. On occasion you become a wing runner, running along and holding the wingtip level until the glider accelerates to a speed where the aerodynamic controls start to function. You even help wash down the club's three sailplanes, which improves their performance in the sky. You get a taste of just about everything that goes on around the gliderport.

Helping hands move a sleek sailplane to the runway.

Club members periodically derig, clean, and inspect the gliders.

One day you get a chance to go out with a ground crew whose duty is to track one of the club members taking a cross-country flight. It's a great experience. It helps familiarize you with the two-way radio communication between crew and pilot. Then, after the pilot is forced to land on an alfalfa field, you get good experience in how to derig, or dismantle, a glider and pack it into a trailer for the journey back to the gliderport.

In a short time, you have learned a lot. You have made new friends, both young and old. All share the same desire to fly. And, although you are the youngest, you are perhaps the most eager to get back into the sky.

5

GOING FLYING

*T*he flight instructor who takes you under his wing is a long-standing member of the Falcon Soaring Club, and is fully FAA certified.

"Listen hard and do what he tells you," Tom says, "and you will be flying solo in no time."

Although the best soaring conditions don't usually begin before ten or eleven in the morning when the ground warms up and thermals begin to form, on the day of your first flying lesson your instructor wants you to get to the gliderport a couple hours ahead of time.

Upon arriving you find that the sailplane you are to use is not just sitting there with its wings spread ready to be flown. Its dismantled parts are packed snugly into a large covered trailer.

You help the instructor extract it piece by piece and put it together. You help bolt the wing halves to the fuselage. You fit the stabilizer onto the tail fin. You work together connecting cables and rods to the proper control surfaces. It takes the two of you a little over a half hour to complete the assembly.

He hands you a clipboard with a list of items on it. "Let's start the preflight," he says.

During the preflight inspection you check every joint, nut, bolt, and hinge. You examine control cable connections. You test the wires and tubes leading to the instruments. You peer into special little windows to take stock of the glider's inner workings. As you move around the aircraft, you keep a sharp eye out for any dents, scratches, or cracks that might have resulted from an earlier flight.

You make sure that mice haven't made a nest in the spoiler slots, and that a spider hasn't taken up housekeeping in the small bore of the *pitot tube* that provides air pressure to operate several of the cockpit instruments. You check that there is battery power for the radio and variometer.

Inspecting spoiler slots for unwanted debris.

You test the tow hook in the nose. You inspect the transparent canopy for cracks or scratches, and pause to wipe it off carefully with plastic cleaner. Coached by your instructor, you get a tire gauge from a pocket in the cockpit and check the air pressure in the landing wheel tire.

Item by item, you mark things off on the checklist . . . things both inside and outside of the cockpit. When you've finished preflighting your glider, your instructor says: "Now let's just stand back and see how she looks."

You wonder what he means. You're quite sure that you haven't missed anything. But you follow him out about fifteen yards, then turn and just stand looking back at the sailplane resting easily on one small wingtip roller.

"How about it?" he asks mysteriously. "Does everything look right? Do you feel she's ready and safe to fly?"

U.S. Air Force Academy cadets preflight their glider. *U.S. Air Force Academy*

After preflighting his aircraft, the pilot stands back and takes an overall view of the vehicle.

Now you think you know what he means. You have inspected the glider, and checked it piece by piece. Now you look at it in total. You see it for what it really is . . . a sensitive, gracefully streamlined aircraft seemingly ready to sail the skies.

"She looks mighty good to me," you say.

"OK, let's go try her out."

After pushing the sailplane over to the end of the runway, you both climb in. You hear him rustling around behind you as he turns knobs to set the altimeter, switches on the battery power, dials in the correct radio frequency, and attends to other prelaunch adjustments.

"You buckled in?" he asks.

You check your seat belt and shoulder harness, pull them snug, and make sure that they are firmly locked in the quick-release buckle located near your lap.

Waiting for a tow plane, a student has time to contemplate her forthcoming lesson.

"Yes, sir," you reply.

The *towplane*, or *tug*, a single-engine light aircraft, taxis up in front of you. It is dragging a two-hundred-foot-long yellow towrope that has a small metal ring on its end. While a volunteer wing runner slips the ring onto the tow hook, your instructor closes and latches the canopy over your heads.

"Just relax and watch what's happening," he says. "I may let you do a little flying after we get upstairs."

With the glider hooked up and checked, the helper moves out and lifts the low wingtip.

The tug pilot pulls forward to take up the slack in the towrope. Then, as you look straight out through the clear canopy, the rudder of the towplane waggles back and forth.

"He's signaling that he's ready," your instructor says. Reflected in the Plexiglas canopy, you see him give the thumbs-up sign to the wing runner. Outside, the runner raises an arm to relay the go-ahead.

You hear the distant dull roar of the tug's engine throttling up. The glider starts accelerating down the asphalt runway. The stick between your knees moves steadily, as do the rudder pedals at your feet. But, as you have been warned before, you are careful to keep clear of them, as the instructor flies the glider from the rear seat.

Then you rivet your attention on the action taking place in front of your eyes. You feel the glider lift gently into the air while the towplane is still on the ground. Your instructor holds it in level flight a mere two or three feet off the runway. Then, as you watch, the towplane leaps into the sky, bobbing in the air currents as it reaches for altitude. As the tug starts turning away from the field, the towrope becomes

The glider lifts off before the towplane.

a curving streak of yellow out beyond the glider's nose.

"How are you doing?" the voice behind you asks calmly.

"Fine, sir. Fine."

As he skillfully tracks behind the towplane, your instructor explains that you are using a *high tow* by holding position a little above the tug propeller's churning wake. Also in a high tow you stay pretty much above the danger zone in case the rope breaks and an end whips back, threatening to foul the glider.

You watch the towplane and rope with great fascination. You are aware of the instructor constantly working the controls in order to follow the towplane's every move.

"You can really mess up on a tow," he explains calmly. "If you get too high above the tug the rope pulls up on its tail, making it nose down. If you get too low you pull its tail down, which can cause the towplane to stall. A tow pilot can get mighty mad if you don't follow behind him properly. He's just apt to cut you loose and let you find your way back home. Tows are not easy. Pay attention."

You do. You watch closely, and sense how each small movement of the controls helps keep the glider tracking behind the towplane.

"Now, then," the instructor says, "see that little string of yarn whipping in the wind in front of you?"

It's the short string that Shana had called a yaw string. You have been aware of it flicking around on the outside of the canopy ever since takeoff. Now your instructor explains its importance. When you fly the glider properly, the head-on airstream keeps the string standing vertically against the windshield. If you let the aircraft's nose swing or yaw sideways from the direction of travel, the string points off at an angle.

"Keep that yaw string centered, and you are flying right,"

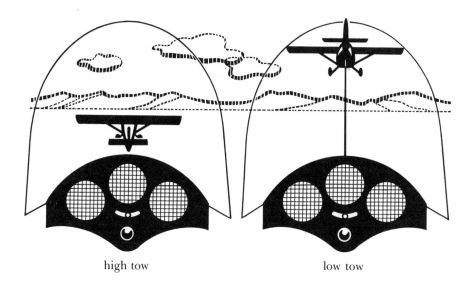

high tow   low tow

Either high tow or low tow keeps the glider out of the tow-plane propeller's turbulent wake. *Soaring Society of America*

he says. "If you see it flutter off to one side, turn in the direction its loose end is pointing, and it will straighten up. You have to keep adjusting controls in order to keep your nose pointed squarely into the airstream."

You begin to wonder when he intends to separate from the towplane. A few seconds later he asks, "What's our altitude?"

You glance at the altimeter. The short needle points between 3 and 4. The long needle points to 6. "Thirty-six hundred feet," you reply, still keeping an eye on the towplane up ahead.

"Good. That's two thousand feet above gliderport elevation. About right. Go ahead, release."

You reach for the red knob poking out from the instrument panel and pull it firmly. You hear a faint click under the glider's nose as the hook springs open. The released towrope snaps free, coiling away. Up ahead the towplane banks sharply down and to the left. At the same time the stick comes back against the inside of your thigh as the instructor veers the sailplane up and to the right . . . free now of all tethers.

Other than a hissing sound of air brushing against the glider's exterior, there is comfortable quiet inside the cockpit. You look down at the patchwork of fields, a cluster of buildings, and the worn paths and roadways of what looks like a miniature world. You have no particular feeling of speed, nor any fear of height.

You glance up and see a scattering of puffy clouds off to the right, as your instructor turns the glider in their direction. You note that the altimeter needle is swinging downward and the sailplane is losing altitude. If you don't find some lift pretty soon, you will need to head back toward the gliderport that is still in sight off to your left. But your instructor doesn't seem worried.

"Want to fly her a while?" he asks.

"Yes, sir," you reply eagerly.

"Put your feet on the rudder pedals. Lightly. Take hold of the stick. Softly. Look out at the *horizon*. Keep it at about eye level. If it starts dropping, ease the stick forward. If it tilts, move the stick toward the low side until it comes level. Keep your indicated airspeed around forty-five miles per hour. That's about right for this plane and the weight we're carrying. Much below it, and you're apt to stall. Always maintain flying speed and watch your yaw string."

It's a big order. While you try to adjust to the pressure on the stick and rudder pedals, the horizon begins dancing around. Every time you try to correct, you overdo it. You imagine the glider fluttering around like a falling leaf. You expect at any moment to feel the instructor take the controls back.

A little left pressure on the stick will level the horizon.

"Not bad," he says from the rear seat. "But relax. Try to use a more gentle touch on the controls. And after each maneuver be sure to center your controls again. Otherwise you will keep rolling or climbing, or whatever. Always bring the controls back to neutral."

You do as he says, and things improve. But you're losing altitude. That worries you. The ground seems closer.

"There should be a thermal under that cloud forming off there to the left," the instructor says. "Let's give it a try. Better let me take over for a few minutes. You can ride the controls so you can feel what I'm doing. But let me do the flying."

You leave your hand and feet lightly on the controls. Soon you are able to anticipate how he will move them as he steers the sailplane toward the distant cloud. As you approach the large gray-bottomed cumulus billowing overhead, the right wing suddenly tilts up. The instructor quickly banks the aircraft toward the high wingtip. Immediately you feel the upsurge of the thermal. The variometer starts to sing. You glance at the instrument. It shows a rate of climb of about five hundred feet a minute.

"We've got a good one!" the instructor says cheerfully. "Hold on to your hat. Here we go."

It's not your hat you are worried about. It's your breakfast. In order to stay within the core of the rising thermal, the instructor puts the glider into a tight banking spiral. The ground spins around below your eyes in a dizzying blur. Nausea begins to nibble at your insides. Oh, boy, don't get sick, you keep telling yourself. You look up from the vortex around which the sailplane is circling. You focus on the sky, and occasionally on the instruments in front of you. You also open the small cockpit vent to let in more cool air.

"You OK?" your instructor asks as he flattens out the spiral a bit.

"I—I'll make it," you reply. And, sure enough, the nausea soon disappears.

You glance at the altimeter, which now indicates 8,200 feet. The thermal has been a strong one. And the vario continues to hum softly, indicating that you are still in lift.

But as the sailplane gets up close to the dark gray base of the cloud, the vario goes silent.

"The thermal has pretty much given out," your instructor says. "But we've got plenty of altitude to play around with for a while. Take over again."

For the next half hour you fly the glider according to his coaching from the rear. You try some S-turns, but can feel the aircraft sideslipping. And the telltale yaw string canted off at an angle proves it.

"Coordinate," your instructor prompts. "Don't try to turn

A two-seated glider, often used as a trainer, sails the sky. *Schweizer Aircraft Corp.*

with just the stick and ailerons. Add a little rudder pressure on the same side you move the stick. Not too much. Rudder and stick together. Gently. And put a little back pressure on the stick to keep the nose from dropping. Check the horizon, bring it level and center the controls. Above all, before you start any turn, *clear the sky*. I haven't seen you looking around lately. Remember, there are other gliders in the air."

So, before you start your next move you swivel your neck and peer all around to be sure no other sailplanes are nearby. After repeated attempts, you start making smooth, coordinated turns, drawing a compliment from the rear seat.

"Good turns are the key to good gliding," he says. "You're

catching on. Cruise around a bit more, then head back for the field."

Ten minutes go by, during which you find yourself feeling more and more at home in the cockpit. The altimeter indicates that you have drifted a bit below two thousand feet above ground level (AGL). You begin to wonder if . . .

"Let's go home," your instructor says, reading your thought. "Try a left-hand landing pattern."

You doubt very much that he intends to let you land the glider. But it's not your place to argue. You have studied landing patterns in ground school. Now you lower the glider's nose and start a slanting crosswind descent toward the right border of the distant gliderport.

You turn and enter the *downwind leg* at an altitude of about seven hundred feet while your instructor keeps silent. At five hundred feet you look off beyond the left wingtip, and mark in your mind a good spot on the airstrip to aim at for touchdown. You check the wind sock and note with satisfaction that you are flying almost directly with the wind, as it should be on the downwind leg.

The tension mounts as you approach the point where you will need to make a turn onto the *base leg*. Maybe he is going to have you land the plane after all. You wonder if you will be able to judge the crosswind and maintain the proper altitude for turning into the *final approach*. You try to relax your grip on the stick, and hold your feet steady on the rudder pedals.

"Nice going," the voice behind you says. "I like a student who doesn't start looking for a way out. But you'd better let me take over now."

With a feeling of relief that you hope doesn't show from the back of your neck, you lift your feet from the rudder pedals, release the stick, and wipe sweaty palms on your pants leg.

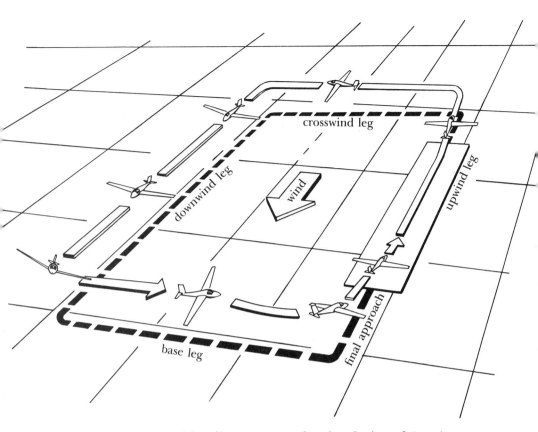

A typical left-hand landing pattern. *Soaring Society of America*

You sigh quietly and relax against the backrest. You feel that it has been a good day. You have done a lot, and learned a lot. But you know that there is a lot more ahead. And you are eager to move on.

6

GETTING IT TOGETHER

*A*fter just three flights with the instructor you begin to feel natural flying a glider. As a junior member of the Falcon Soaring Club, you are ready to claim your piece of the sky.

But it takes some thought and planning. A flight instructor usually gets paid for giving lessons, and there are club dues to think about, as well as aero tow charges.

Fortunately, your instructor, a past president of the club, has his own business in town. He flies sailplanes as a hobby. If you will pay your own tow fees, attend meetings, help with ground crewing, do your full share of whatever work needs doing around the club and its sailplanes, and show real interest, he is willing to donate his teaching time.

"You can't beat that," Shana observes at one of the meetings. "That, and the fellowship of learning together and sharing experiences, is one of the advantages of joining a gliding club."

As time goes by, your instructor becomes more demanding. He counts on you to study on your own time. There are lots of helpful SSA publications in the club library, plus assorted other books and pamphlets about everything from meteorology to navigation and all phases of airwork. You spend hours poring over them. You soon learn answers to questions you think your instructor will ask before each flight.

"Remember what we discuss," he cautions. "Someday when you go for your private pilot's license, you will be grilled by an FAA inspector. He or she will also take you up for a check flight. He or she won't take it easy on you."

You improve with each flight. Then, one day after you have preflighted the glider and settled into the front seat, your instructor climbs in behind you, hooks up, and says, "She's all yours."

A line boy hooks up the towrope . . .

. . . then acts as a wing runner.

After completing all your cockpit checks, you close the canopy and signal to Tom, who is acting as wing runner, to hook up the rope. You test the release and hook the rope up again. After an exchange of rudder-wagging signals, the towplane pilot feeds throttle to the engine and surges forward. After running along for about a dozen yards, Tom lets go of the wingtip. As acceleration increases, the controls harden as rudder and ailerons bite into the swift airstream. With deft movements of stick and rudder pedals, you keep the wings level. Upon reaching flying speed, you pull back on the stick to lift the glider off the ground. Immediately you level off and skim just above the asphalt until the towplane reaches its own flying speed and takes off on the far end of the rope.

From then on, as the tug's pilot points his plane's nose skyward, it's a game of follow-the-leader. Despite the plane's bobbing and weaving in the unstable air, you try to hold position above the propeller's wake. At the same time you try to keep the horizon reasonably level, and the yaw string centered.

Even in high tow you don't escape all of the turbulent wake stirred up by the tug. You keep moving the stick and rudder pedals in an almost desperate effort to fly formation on the towplane. When it climbs, you climb. When it turns, you follow. You try to anticipate and not over-control. You work to keep the rope reasonably taut without pulling the tug's tail out of line. You also guard against allowing too much slack in the rope. Often, when excess slack is taken up sharply, the rope snaps, sending the frayed end whipping back at the glider.

By the time you feel that you are in full control of the tow, the pilot has brought you over an old stone quarry, where heat usually radiates from a large jumbled field of rocky discards. You can even see a small cu forming out ahead, and high. You check the altimeter. Approximately two thousand feet above ground level.

It's time to release. You reach forward and pull the knob. As soon as you are free of the tug, you aim toward the cu.

When you reach the invisible edge of the thermal and feel the right wingtip bob up, you bank toward it, and immediately go into a climbing spiral to stay within the column of rising air. Riding nature's elevator upward, you feel as though wings are sprouting from your own shoulders. You have gotten over the tendency to lean away from the banked turn, as though fearful that the glider will roll on over. Now you simply relax, let your body follow the plane's movement, and glory in the view laid out beyond the transparent bubble around your head.

You leave the thermal at six thousand feet, clear the air

around you, and try a couple of stalls. You pull back on the stick, climbing gradually until the glider loses vertical flying speed. The normal wind sounds die out. The controls become sluggish, since there is not enough velocity in the airstream to operate rudder, elevator, or ailerons. The stick wobbles loosely in your hand. The aircraft trembles like a sick bird about to fall. The glider stalls and the nose drops. The sinking feel of danger makes the hair rise on the nape of your neck. But there are no helpful words from the rear seat.

To recover, you shove the stick forward. The glider starts to fall off on one wing, so you push the rudder pedal on the high side to prevent a *spin*. With the lowered nose, gravity helps you start to regain flying speed. When the wind begins to hiss against the wing and canopy, you pull back on the stick and level off before losing too much altitude.

"Good enough," your instructor comments behind you. "Up here at high altitude stalls are no problem. Just don't let it happen at low altitude where there isn't room to recover before you hit the ground. Now that you know how to handle stalls, make it a practice to stay away from them whenever you can."

Other days and other flights follow. You practice takeoffs and landings, dives and climbs, stalls and spins, turns and more turns. You learn how to avoid or make use of a sideslip, which occurs when you use too much aileron and not enough rudder. You learn to turn without skidding, which happens when you use too much rudder and not enough aileron. In time, you find that you are moving the controls almost without thinking, instinctively.

Landing still poses a major challenge. Sometimes you just ride the controls while the instructor performs the final landing. But each time he has you fly the glider a little closer to the touchdown point.

With practice, a glider pilot begins to feel that he is part of the aircraft. *Schweizer Aircraft Corp.*

Then, one day after finishing a good session of thermaling within sight of the gliderport, he says, "Take her in."

"All the way?"

"All the way."

You straighten up a bit in your cushioned seat, and wiggle the controls to convince yourself that he has really turned them over to you. Then, as you have been so carefully taught, you clear the sky to be sure no other gliders are nearby. You check the altimeter. Nosing down slightly, you keep the airspeed a bit above the normal cruising speed just to be on the safe side and avoid a possible stall. And again you check the horizon to be sure the wings are level.

You make a gentle banking turn and head for the glider-port, which you judge to be about six miles away. As you approach the field, you make sure the sky is clear around you once again.

Entering the traffic pattern, you note by the orange wind sock that a mild quartering crosswind is blowing right to left over the airfield.

You enter the pattern a little high. But better high than low, since it's easier to lose altitude than try to gain it. You use the spoilers to slow down and help lop off a couple of hundred feet as you enter the downwind leg. You check the airspeed indicator to be sure you are maintaining good flying speed.

In the downwind leg you retract the spoilers and apply a little right stick and rudder to keep the crosswind from pushing you off your course. Halfway through the downwind leg you glance straight off to your left and mentally mark your touchdown target on the landing strip, just this side of a yellow glider parked on the far side of the ramp.

At an altitude of approximately five hundred feet, you bank left onto the base leg and approach the end of the landing strip at a 90-degree angle.

"Still too high," you warn yourself as you make your next turn, line up with the runway, and start your final approach. You know you have to kill off some altitude or you may overshoot the field.

You sight ahead, glimpse the yellow glider parked off to the side, and focus on your planned touchdown point. But even as you aim toward it, the small area slips from sight beneath the glider's nose. You pull the lever to pop the spoilers again to slow your approach and help you lose some altitude. The touchdown point floats back into view.

You concentrate your gaze outside of the cockpit. As the end of the runway slips past a dozen feet beneath the wing, you start your *flare* by pulling back on the stick. The nose comes up level and seems to hang there. As though it doesn't want to come down, the glider floats on a bubble of air a few feet above the warm asphalt. Just right. You hold it there, nose slightly up, until the aircraft loses flying speed and settles to the ground.

You let it roll a few yards, then pull full back on the spoiler handle to set the wheel brake, and come to a stop.

As the glider tips onto its small protective wingtip wheel, you lean back and take a deep breath. Except for a bit of a bounce on landing, you feel that you have not done too shabby a job of flying. You only hope that your instructor shares the feeling.

"Nicely done," he compliments from the rear. "You probably know that you could have swung out and done a couple of S-turns to kill off some of the excess altitude you had coming into the final approach. But you made good use of your spoilers. You're getting there."

You spend the next few flying lessons steadily increasing your skills. Now and then your flight instructor springs an emergency on you. Several times he puts the glider into a spin, then turns the controls over to you. Or he sits back and tells you to make a ticklish crosswind landing.

Then, one day when you haven't paid particular attention to how far you have strayed from the gliderport, or just where you are, he suddenly barks a mock emergency at you, "Take her down. Now!"

Then he remains silent, while every fiber in your body and mind springs alert. You are able to make out a couple of familiar landmarks. You consult your compass, and turn in the direction that you think, or hope, the gliderport is located. But you are down to nearly two thousand feet of altitude when you spot it through the haze. You set up an emergency plan that you hope will stretch your glide enough to reach the runway. Otherwise you will have to make an off-field landing, which can be very touchy.

Hoarding your altitude as best you can, and stretching your glide to the utmost, you manage to reach the runway and make a safe landing.

"You handled that pretty well," your flight instructor says after you have unbuckled and climbed out of the glider. "But I had the feeling that you weren't very sure of where you were or what you were doing at first. Always stay sharp. You never know when conditions may force you to make an off-field landing. You may have to come down on some pasture, mesa, road, or other emergency landing spot. Sooner or later most glider pilots are faced with having to *land out*. So you must always be prepared."

You get the message. And, although you will try to avoid it, you will not let the possibility of having to make an off-field landing scare you unduly.

After letting it sink in a little, the instructor turns to you. "You've been doing fine," he says, smiling. "Are you ready for the big one?"

"Have I really earned my student pilot license?" you ask hopefully.

"Some time ago," he says. "I've already ordered your FAA certificate. Can you guess what's next?"

You pretty well know what he's getting to. A delightful tingle zips along your spine.

"You . . . you mean solo?"

"Solo," he replies.

7

SOLO

A few days later you meet your instructor in the operations shack. You try to appear cool and calm. But your insides are churning. You hope that this is the day he will let you solo. The day that you will become the pilot-in-command of your aircraft. The lone eagle!

However, your instructor seems to be in no hurry. He asks to see your logbook. He spends several minutes going over the carefully kept records of each of your flights. Not only does the logbook contain the detailed history of your progress as a glider pilot, but it is always subject to review by the FAA. And later, when you visit other clubs or gliderports, your logbook will testify to your experience as a glider pilot. You also have to show it if you want to rent a glider.

After handing back your book that carefully logs twenty-three flights spread over a little more than eight hours of flying time, your instructor turns to the flying business of the day. He leads you to the bulletin board, where the latest weather forecast sheets are posted. He points out the highs and lows and the frontal action showing on the Weather Bureau charts. "It looks promising," he says. "When it warms up there should be some decent lift. All you have to do is find it."

He moves over to an area map pinned to a nearby wall. He quizzes you to see if you recognize important landmarks. He has you point out several possible emergency landing sites, just in case you have to make an off-field landing. Apparently your answers satisfy him, for he claps you on the shoulder and says, "Let's go."

But it seems that he's not quite ready to turn you loose alone in a sailplane. When you reach the waiting glider, he suggests that the two of you take a little check flight together. "Just to be sure that the machine is airworthy," he says.

Well, you can see the updated *airworthiness certificate* posted in the cockpit next to the glider's registration certificate. You suspect that the flight instructor is not as interested in the glider's airworthiness as he is in yours. You get busy at once preflighting the aircraft, as you have been taught. By the time you are finished, the instructor has already settled in the back seat. You climb in front, make your cockpit checks, and buckle up.

As you reach up to close the *canopy*, you ask, "You want me to fly her, sir?"

"Absolutely. Show me what you can do."

You wish he hadn't said it quite that way. But you set about to show him, anyway. You manage to follow the tow-plane in good style. You release in an area that usually spawns strong thermals. But, discouragingly, you fail to find one. What a way to start the day. With the variometer showing steady sink, you adjust your gliding speed to get the best distance out of the sailplane's L/D glide ratio of 25:1. It provides you about ten minutes of gliding time before you must commit yourself to a landing. You run through some shallow turns while still searching for some kind of an updraft. Without lift, you won't be able to show your instructor much. And the glider continues descending.

Buckled up, instructor and student are ready to close the canopy and head skyward. *U.S. Air Force Academy*

"No lift," you say finally.

"Mostly my fault," he says. "It's too early. We should have waited a while longer, and given things a chance to heat up. Guess you better take her in."

You turn the nose back toward the gliderport, descend into the landing pattern, and touch down softly. You secure the aircraft on the parking ramp before making your way to the snack bar. You and your instructor sit for an hour over donuts and milk discussing sailplaning in general.

Meanwhile, the airfield gets busy with gliders taking off and landing. Your instructor scans the sky.

"Things look a lot better out there," he says. "There are even a few cu's forming over near the canyons. You want to try it now?"

"Yes, sir," you reply eagerly.

Back at the glider, you don't forget your training. You

make another complete preflight check before climbing in. You are all hooked up before it dawns on you that your instructor is still standing outside. He shows no sign of intending to get in.

"She's all yours," he says simply. Then he turns and walks away as you try to keep your emotions under control.

You consult the chart posted on the instrument panel, and adjust the elevator *trim tab* a bit to balance the glider's *center of gravity (CG)* to allow for the reduced weight distribution due to the empty rear seat. You will fine-tune the trim when you get in the air and see how the glider flies.

Climbing out on tow is bumpy. You need all your skill at the controls in order to hold position behind the pitching tug. Then, at two thousand feet AGL, you reach for the red knob and pull. Nothing happens. The long yellow rope still stretches out between you and the towplane. You jerk the knob again. Still nothing! Of all the times for the hook to jam!

Panic nibbles at you. Although the tug pilot can release his end of the rope if need be, you don't like the thought of him leaving you with a couple of hundred feet of loose towrope whipping around your glider. In addition to the burden of extra weight and drag, there is the risk of the rope snagging on trees, fences, or any number of other ground objects when you are trying to land.

You jerk the knob again. The hook still doesn't release. By now you imagine the tug pilot is wondering what's going on. He knows that this is your first solo attempt. He may think that you have frozen at the controls. You deliberate whether to rock your wings vigorously, and move the glider out to the side. It is the standard signal that the hook is stuck. But you hate the idea of having to declare any kind of an emergency on your first solo flight.

Tracking behind the towplane is a tense part of any flight.

You ease the stick forward and drop down into the towplane's churning wake. Perhaps the vibration of the added turbulence will help jar the hook open. It doesn't work. You hit the rudder pedal, yaw sharply to the left, and pull the knob once again. Still nothing. At any moment you expect the tug pilot to release his end of the rope, and leave it for you to worry about. But before giving up, you yaw to the right, and jerk the knob still one more time.

Clack!

As the hook opens, the rope immediately snaps forward away from the glider's nose. Freed suddenly of the glider's weight, the tug banks down and away. You make a climbing right turn.

You take a few moments to gather your wits, and force the incident from your mind. There will be time later to find out why the hook jammed.

Detecting that you have to keep a little back pressure on the stick to maintain level flight, you adjust the trim tab until the glider is so finely balanced that it almost flies itself. Then you set out to complete your *task*, the name by which a glider mission is known. There are other sailplanes in the area. You frequently clear the sky to be sure there is plenty of open space around you.

Your variometer remains glumly silent. You are not finding any lift. A glance at the altimeter shows a slow but steady loss of altitude. But you are still well within gliding range of the airstrip, so you are not worried. Still, you would like to make your first solo flight . . . or at least the remainder of it . . . a good one. You keep looking around for signs of thermal activity, or perhaps a decent updraft over near the hills. The latter seems unlikely, since you don't see any wings flashing in the sun above the ridges.

Then, about two miles away, and well above your present altitude, you see three gliders wheeling in slow climbing circles. You check your chart. A thermal must be forming above Buzzard Mesa. It's a reasonable guess. By now the treeless rocky area would be heating up and starting to radiate a thermal. In fact, a telltale cu is just starting to blossom above the circling gliders.

You lose more precious altitude en route to joining the others. You are careful not to let the airfield slip out of gliding range. Approaching beneath the others, you notice the direction they are circling. When your left wingtip bobbles, you turn toward it, and enter the thermal.

Having ample lift, the glider pilot can relax in the cockpit.
Schweizer Aircraft Corp.

The vario now begins to hum its welcome tune. You see the needle rise to indicate six hundred feet a minute of strong lift.

For the next few minutes you continue circling upward like a hawk. Now and then you widen the circle to check the diameter of the rising air column. When the vario stops humming, you know you've reached the edge, and immediately duck back inside.

Most important, you keep a constant lookout for the other sailplanes that are sharing the thermal. A couple of the gliders have already reached the upper limits of the cu's lift and have gone off in search of other updrafts.

You check your watch. You have been up about thirty-five minutes. You know that other members are waiting on the ground for a turn at the club glider before the heat of the day begins to wane.

You give yourself another fifteen minutes to use up most of your altitude. As you descend you practice assorted maneuvers. You don't try anything fancy for fear that your instructor might be watching you through field glasses and accuse you of hotdogging.

When you get back down to two thousand feet, you steer toward the gliderport and start setting up for a landing. You kill off another thousand feet by the time you check the wind sock and turn downwind for the first leg of the landing pattern. You are still a little high when you turn left onto the base leg. You pop the spoilers as you swing left once again and enter the final approach. You come down steeply over a bordering row of young trees, and flare out about four feet above the runway. You hold the glider in a level float, using partial spoilers until it settles to the ground with barely a

Skimming the ground in a slightly nose-up flare and then . . .

. . . touching down.

bounce. You let it roll toward the group of waiting club members before you apply the brake.

No sooner do you unbuckle and step out onto the parking apron than they swarm around to congratulate you on your first solo flight.

It is, indeed, an occasion for celebration. And early in the festivities you feel a tug on the back of your shirt, followed by the sound of scissors snipping. Then someone hands you your cut-off shirttail. It is all part of the traditional ceremony accorded a flier who has just made his first solo flight.

Grinning through it all, you swear that you will hang on to that shirttail for the rest of your life.

8

CROSS-COUNTRY FLIGHT

*D*uring the next few months you gain soaring experience on short flights both with and without your instructor. One day an FAA examiner checks you out on your general sailplaning abilities, and quizzes you on Federal Aviation Regulations.

As a member of the Soaring Society of America, you reach various levels of achievement. After your first solo flight you are awarded SSA's A pin. This is followed shortly thereafter by the B pin after you have been tested for your overall proficiency and knowledge of sailplaning. Finally you receive a C pin, having three stylized white gulls flying formation across its sky-blue background, to vouch that you are ready to take on cross-country flying.

You now boast an SSA serial number. Your name and achievements have been listed in *Soaring* magazine, which is read by virtually all members of the society. Much to your pleasure, you have become a true member of the somewhat exclusive fraternity of thermal sniffers.

After several short- and medium-range flights of twenty or so miles in the club's sleek single-seat fiberglass high-performance glider, you get the urge to spread your wings,

Careful study of maps and charts precedes any cross-country flight.

get away from the local area, and go cross-country.

You pore over maps and government sectional charts. You lay out a proposed course that goes eastward from Hillcrest to Juniper Grove. Then it swings northwest to an old military training airfield that is sometimes used by weekend fliers. The final leg stretches southwest back to the Hillcrest gliderport. The total route comes to about sixty-five miles. With decent thermals and few headwinds, you should be able to make it in two to three hours. You show the flight plan to your instructor, who still oversees your flying activities.

"That's a pretty ambitious task," he says without actually objecting. "Do you figure that you have had enough experience with navigation and all that?"

"Yes, sir."

"Do you have a *crew* lined up?"

"Tom and Shana said they would crew for me," you reply.

"Good. Get plenty of sleep Friday night. I'll be here to see you off."

That Saturday you arrive at the field at about nine in the morning. It promises to be a warm day. Traces of cumulus clouds are already forming like a field of cauliflower above the nearby ridge of hills.

To bolster your hopes for a good soaring day, you telephone the local Flight Service Station for the latest weather data and a short-term forecast. The report is promising.

With an orange felt marker you trace your proposed route on a regular road map, plus the sectional chart. You fold them systematically so you won't have to wrestle with them later in the tight cockpit.

You preflight your aircraft. You double-check that you have put a canteen of water aboard, plus some food to nibble on. You carry a jackknife and a small pocket compass, just in case you land out in some remote wilderness area. You clean your sunglasses, and slip your logbook and pencil into a cockpit compartment.

Since parachutes are required for cross-country flying, and you have been trained to use one, your instructor helps you buckle one on.

"You still want to go for the whole sixty-five miles?" he asks.

"I'd like to," you say. "I can always turn back."

"If you know when to do it," he warns. "Just be careful. Think. And good luck."

By the time everything has been checked out and made ready, the sun is high overhead.

While waiting for the towplane, you review the route with Tom and Shana. You mark the two turnpoints on their map—one above the water pumping plant just outside Juniper Grove; the other at the rickety old hangar of the

Wearing a parachute is a rule of safety for cross-country soaring.

abandoned military training field. You give them the general compass headings that you intend to follow on each leg of the triangular course.

"Got film in the camera?" Tom asks, pointing to the small still camera mounted rigidly on the edge of the cockpit inside the canopy. Its lens focuses off beyond the left wingtip. When you bank around each turnpoint, you will snap a couple of pictures of the pumping plant and old hangar to help prove where you have been. You also carry a sealed *barograph* to record your entire flight. Both are standard procedures for cross-country flights.

"Try to keep in radio contact with us," Tom says. "There's a lot of open space out there. We don't want to lose you."

Circling birds often mark an inviting thermal.

"Roger," you reply as the canopy comes down over your head. You settle yourself as comfortably as you can in the confined cockpit.

During the tow up to altitude you get bounced around in the unstable air that marks strong weather conditions. At an altitude of about nineteen hundred feet, you spot a likely thermal area over to your right, and pull the rope release.

No sooner are you on your own than you run into unexpected sink. You look around for the thermal you had anticipated, but you can't find it. Then far to your right you spot a couple of birds—hawks or vultures, you can't tell which—soaring in lazy circles. You stretch your glide until you are directly beneath them, and you feel the upward surge as the glider enters the thermal. The variometer lets out a welcome squeal. You spiral within the thermal's core and are suddenly startled to be staring eye to eye at one of the soaring birds. It's a red-tailed hawk. Then, with a squawk and a ruffle of feathers, it flashes out of view.

You continue on upward until at seventy-two hundred feet you reach cloud base, and the thermal flattens out. You point the sailplane's nose eastward in a flat glide and start reaching for distance. Still, while stretching your glide you lose about three thousand feet by the time you find another thermal. Luckily it's a good one, and you are soon back up to eighty-three hundred feet. You check your compass, and, holding to a general heading, glide toward the next thermal. You work its lift, then move on to the next. Out ahead, cumulus are strung out one after another to form a regular cloud street. Delighted, you ride along it all the way to Juniper Grove. At the turnpoint, you bank sharply to the left

By two-way radio, pilot and crew try to keep in touch during a cross-country flight.

so that your wingtip is aimed down at the pumping plant. Quickly you snap a couple of photos with the stationary camera. Then, as you straighten out and take a north-westerly heading, you reach for your radio mike.

"Glider two-seven-Tango to crew. Come in. Over."

There's a moment's pause, then, "Crew to two-seven-Tango. Go ahead. Over."

"I turned the corner at Juniper Grove. Looks like good lift to the north. I'm heading for turnpoint two via Bascomb Ridge and Three Corners. Over."

"Roger. We don't have you in sight. But we'll do our best to follow. Try to stick close to some road. There's a lot of untamed desert out where you're headed. You sure you want to go for it? Over."

"Affirmative," you say. "See you back at Hillcrest before sundown. Two-seven-Tango. Out."

As you switch off the radio, you wonder if maybe you are overreaching a bit on your first real cross-country flight. You might even have sounded a little cocky. But it could be months before you might again run into such promising soaring conditions. You just want to make the most of your good fortune.

As you fly your northerly leg you check off several landmarks that you have circled on your sectional chart. You nose slightly into a quartering breeze in order to stay on course. You even find time to whistle a little tune.

And, without realizing it, you are also backing yourself into a corner! You first become aware of it when you look out toward the horizon only to discover that much of the cloud street seems to have evaporated, and you find yourself surrounded by large patches of blue sky and no lift. Making it worse, you suddenly hit an area of sink, and the variometer needle drops sharply.

You now become concerned over what lies beneath you.

Earlier there had seemed to be plenty of clearings in sight in case you needed to land out. Now you discover with alarm that everything below is brush-covered and rocky. Terrain that could destroy a glider.

To make it worse, a headwind starts slowing you down. Suddenly alert, you know that you must act quickly. You realize that, in the pleasure of the flight, you have paid too little attention to some of the things you were taught. You are particularly startled by the realization that you have neglected to heed the glider pilot's first law of survival. You have not made sure that there was always at least one suitable landing site within easy gliding range of your aircraft. Certainly you do not see one now!

Fighting off panic, you feel your best choice is to go on. As you turn and aim hopefully toward a small cluster of clouds, you unfold your chart and check in all directions for a possible landing sight. The most promising seems to be a small dry lake that looks to be about twelve miles away and fairly straight ahead. It is marked Cottontail Dry Lake. But right now, without some added lift, it is well out of range.

You try to make radio contact with your crew. You get a weak, static-filled answer. Although garbled, within the radio's crackling reply you detect certain agitation and a note of warning in the few words you can make out. Perhaps you have overreached, perhaps you have been a bit careless, but there is no time to waste on regrets.

In growing desperation, you scan the horizon. You notice a line of low hills off to your right. A decent breeze blowing up their sides might yield some ridge lift running along the crest. It's worth a try.

At an altitude of thirty-one hundred feet, you head hopefully toward the hills. You look for smoke, blowing dust, any sign of a favorable wind gusting up the slope. You see nothing.

You switch on your radio and try to contact your crew. There is no answer to your urgent call. They are either out of radio range or behind some high ground that blocks out the signal. If you can't reach them, they won't know where to look for you if you have to make an off-field landing, which seems likely.

As far as you can see around you, the country is totally uninhabited. Before reaching the shadow of the hills, where you still hope to find enough ridge lift to carry you on, you switch radio frequencies and try one more call.

"Glider two-seven-Tango. I can't raise my crew, and may have to land out. Come in, anybody. Over."

Shortly, within a bit of electronic static, you hear a welcome voice. "Two-seven-Tango. This is eight-six-Sierra. I'm over Baldy Mountain. Can I help? Over."

"I've run out of lift," you say. And as you talk you search your map for Baldy Mountain. You locate it about eight miles back beyond your left shoulder. It just might be that someone over Baldy would be high enough to make radio contact with your crew. "Would you try to relay word to my crew on frequency 123.5? Over."

"I read you, two-seven-Tango. What's your location and heading? Over."

You give him the details, as near as you know them.

"Roger, two-seven-Tango. Good luck. Eight-six-Sierra, out."

Having abandoned all thoughts of going on toward turn-point two, you wet your dry throat with a swig of water from your canteen. As you get closer to the hills, you can make out trees quivering in the wind, and patches of long grass rippling upward along the slopes. Both are good signs, and you drop down toward the near ridge. As you arrive at the windward edge, the upward glancing breeze pushes like an unseen hand on the underside of the glider.

You ride the lift along the ridge for all it is worth. Meanwhile you abandon any hope of reaching the cumulus activity that you notice taking place in the distance. You will rely on the ridge lift for two or three more miles.

But, just as things are looking better, your hopes are dashed. Without warning, the ridge bends away from under your glider, and the hills flatten out. Suddenly all ridge lift ceases. There is now nowhere to go but down.

Desperately, you look off into the valley below. Ahead and off to your left, you can just make out the tan-colored smudge of what you believe to be Cottontail Dry Lake. Judging its distance against your altitude, you feel there is hope of making it—providing that you don't run into more headwind or some unexpected sink conditions.

Despite a frantic search for something closer, you can see no other place below where you could safely land. A narrow, winding dirt road off to your right offers little hope for landing your long-winged craft.

Tensely, and with occasional glances at the airspeed indicator, you ease back on the stick to stretch your glide toward the dry lake. While still a mile from the light brown patch of clay, you wonder if you can make it. You certainly are lower than you had hoped to be.

You make a final appeal over your radio—just in case anyone happens to be within hearing range.

With no altitude to spare, you aren't able to overfly the lake bed, look it over, and set up a proper landing pattern. You simply point the glider's nose at the distant brown smudge. As you get close, you can make out the spiderweb pattern of cracks in the smooth dry clay surface. Detecting a slight crosswind drift of your aircraft, you abandon the luxury of following a standard landing pattern. You swing onto what you hope will be a proper upwind final approach. As the mesquite bushes bordering the clay oval start reaching

Waiting for a retrieve after landing out.

up at your wings, you stretch your glide as best you can without losing critical flying speed. As you skim over the last of the bushes, you pop the spoilers and pull the nose up in a flare a scant three feet above the cracked clay. You apply a little right rudder to keep a sudden gust of wind from drifting you into the mesquite.

The heat coming off the dry lake surface keeps you floating just off the ground. You put a little back pressure on the stick until, on the edge of a stall, the sailplane settles to the ground. You let it coast for a dozen or so yards, then apply the brake, and stop.

With one wingtip resting on the ground, you sit for a minute, breathing deeply and letting your pulse slow down a bit. Then you unlatch the canopy, release your buckles, and step out. Having forgotten enough rules and made enough mistakes for one day, you figure that you had better start preparing for what could be a long wait.

You have barely finished thinking about your next step when you are relieved to see a streak of dust rising from the narrow dirt road that you had barely noticed during your straight-in landing approach. In a couple of minutes a sheriff's marked vehicle races across the lake bed and skids to a dusty stop in front of the glider. A young officer leaps out.

"Are you OK?" he asks. "I heard your radio call for help."

"I'm fine," you assure him. "So is the glider."

"Guess it's your lucky day," he says, slipping a notebook out of his pocket. "I have to make out a little report. Mind a few questions?"

You've barely gotten into the answers when another dust plume appears. Moments later the familiar van rumbles

Sheriff and crew arrive within minutes of each other.

The glider is dismantled and tucked into its trailer for the journey home.

across the dry lake bed pulling the glider trailer behind it. Although you suspect that Tom and Shana will be less than pleased with the day's events, at least you are relieved to know that eight-six-Sierra was able to relay your message of distress.

You take a deep breath and wait for them to arrive. Suddenly you are bone weary, as the tension of the past couple of hours takes its toll. Almost numbly, you realize that you have made a few mistakes of judgment that you are determined never to repeat.

Yet despite the touchy moments you feel that you functioned fairly well in the crisis. You admit to yourself that you even relished the excitement and adventure of the flight. And, most important, you did manage to bring the glider—and yourself—down without a scratch.

Surely, there will be other flights in the future . . . better-planned and better-piloted flights. You will see to that. Meanwhile, you are not likely to forget your first attempt at cross-country soaring.

$\mathscr{O}\!\!\!-\!\!\!9$

FUN AND COMPETITION

*A*s with other forms of active sport, once you have learned the art and science of soaring, there are joys to be shared and goals to be reached. Some are personal goals by which you measure your flying talents. Others involve friendly gatherings in which groups of sailplane pilots share the fun and excitement of competition.

This, of course, does not discount the fact that once you become a skilled and experienced glider pilot much of your air time will be used in going aloft and exploring the sheer almost spiritual delights of soaring high over the heads of more earthbound mortals.

Sailplaning for either personal pleasure or competition usually involves three elements of flight—how high, how fast, or how far can you go?

A long list of awards and notices of achievement constantly entice you to improve on your gliding skills. At various levels of learning you receive awards through the SSA, which operates as a division of the *National Aeronautics Association* (NAA). The NAA serves as the governing body for aviation contests within the United States. In turn, both the SSA and NAA cooperate with the *Federation Aeronautique*

Competition tests how high, fast, or far a sailplane pilot can soar.

Internationale (FAI). The FAI supervises flying competition on a global basis, and keeps the main body of records. Headquartered in France, the major award requirements as established by the FAI are standardized the world over. To become official, any record flying achievement, be it power plane or glider, must be recognized by the FAI.

Having this central authority means that in order to have his or her flying accomplishment accepted in the circle of sailplaners, the glider pilot in West Germany must complete the same tasks as the thermal rider in New Mexico or Japan. Hence, as you earn FAI badges, which progress from fairly easy to very difficult, you not only gain respect from your local soaring friends but you also earn certain global renown.

Near the beginning of your training, you earned your A, B, and C pins for your assorted skills in handling a glider on the ground as well as in the air. You demonstrated knowledge of aerodynamics, meteorology, and gliderport procedures. You convinced the FAA examiner that you are well aware of standard flying regulations, and respect numerous rules of safety. You have admitted making mistakes during your first major cross-country attempt. But you are relieved to find that no one keeps holding them up to you.

Now, determined to plan future tasks more carefully and not try too much in a single flight, you prepare for the next venture. In looking over the various ways by which you can earn FAI-recognized awards, you find that they become increasingly difficult with each goal you set for yourself.

Having received your C pin, you study the FAI requirements for pursuing the Silver Badge. In appearance, it resembles the C pin, except it has a leafy silver wreath around it. Hence, sometimes it is called a Silver C badge.

To earn the Silver Badge requires three separate tasks. You must make a soaring flight of at least five hours duration. You must fly a distance of not less than 31.2 miles (50 kilometers) in a straight line . . . at least in a single direction; for the vagaries of finding lift along the way seldom allow a sailplane to glide in a straight line for very long. The third requirement toward earning the silver is to gain at least

3,280 feet (1,000 meters) of altitude after being released from the tow vehicle. You are not allowed to complete more than two of these three tasks in a single flight.

Next comes the Gold Badge, with its gold rather than silver wreath around it. Earning the gold involves similar but more difficult tasks than those required for the silver . . . at least in two instances. Actually, you can apply the five-hour duration flight that helped get you the silver toward earning your Gold Badge. But the distance requirement increases to making a cross-country flight of at least 187 miles (300 kilometers). You must also achieve an altitude gain from your lowest point after release of at least 9,843 feet (3,000 meters).

It is all possible, you tell yourself confidently. In fact, more than two thousand SSA members, past and present, can boast having earned Gold Badges.

Adding Diamonds to the Gold Badge is like reaching for the stars, and, in many cases, touching them. If good enough, you can earn as many as three Diamonds. To have one Diamond set into the gold wreath, you must fly to a preselected and announced goal, and return to your starting point. The total distance must be at least 187 miles. Since you are required to reach a definite target, this task takes meticulous planning. You need a thorough knowledge of weather movements, the ability to seek and find needed lift along the way, and, of course, luck.

You also can earn a Diamond by sailplaning a sheer distance of at least 310.7 miles (500 kilometers). It can be in a straight line, over a triangular course, a roundtrip out-and-return flight, or a dog leg with just one turning point.

You will have to provide proof of each accomplishment, such as photographs taken at turning points or witness accounts, and in all cases you will need to carry a sealed bar-

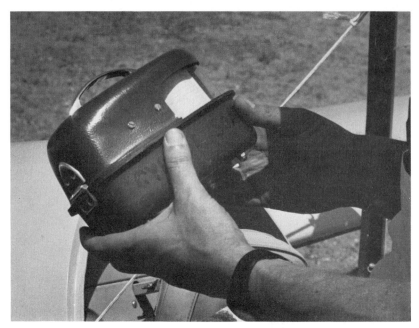

A sealed barograph records the glider's flight . . .

. . . on a special sensitized tape.

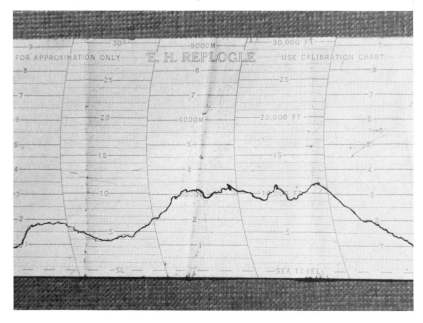

ograph to trace the flight on special coated paper, which you submit to the SSA for evaluation. A distance Diamond is a tough task, no matter how you cut it. You must be in top physical condition, for you will spend most of a day cramped into a small cockpit. You will need to master navigation, meteorology, and the aerodynamics of your particular aircraft, and make good use of your maps and compass. You will also need to carry drinking water and some high-protein food for stamina, and make whatever other preparations that may be necessary for a long flight.

To add a third Diamond to your Gold Badge you must soar to an altitude of 16,404 feet (5,000 meters) above your point of release. This puts you well into the area where you risk oxygen starvation, or *hypoxia*. But the hazard is minimal, since you will take oxygen and a mask with you.

You also must wear proper clothing to combat the cold you will encounter at high altitudes. And, of course, you must have the piloting skill and steady nerves needed for exploring this rarefied atmosphere.

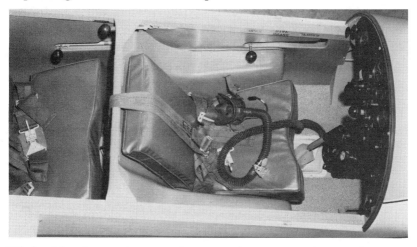

High altitude soaring requires wearing an oxygen mask. *Schweizer Aircraft Corp.*

But when you finally possess a Gold Badge with three Diamonds set into its border, you become a member of soaring's elite few.

Earning pins, badges, and diamonds are tests of your personal soaring proficiency. There are additional ways that you can enter into the fun and challenge of competing against others. Throughout the year, but particularly during spring and summer months, when the sun heats the earth to spawn upwelling currents of warm air, all kinds of competitive glider meets take place across the country. Some are spur-of-the-moment one-day meets. Others are well-organized and advertised affairs that may last a week or more.

You can start with club or interclub competition, where the main challenge is to determine who can fly faster, farther, or higher than any of the others in whatever weather conditions exist that day. It's a test of flying skill, plus how good you are at locating and using whatever local lift nature offers.

Most large, organized soaring meets are sanctioned by the SSA. They include state competitions, regional meets that take in several states, and an annual national championship. Every two years a dozen or so superior glider pilots from around the world are invited to compete in the World Gliding Championships. The World event is held at some renowned FAI-approved soaring site most anywhere on earth. He or she who accumulates the most points during the days of competition is crowned champion thermal sniffer, ridge lift rider, and wave soarer of the globe. And you try not to lose sight of the fact that, if you give it enough time and effort, someday that crown might be yours.

In most meets the events are broken down into glider classes in order to equalize the competition. Although there are apt to be some in-between categories, competition gliders fit generally into three major classes—standard, sports, and open.

In standard class events you fly the less expensive, but safe and comfortable, sailplanes that appeal to the typical weekend soaring enthusiast. Most clubs have at least one standard class glider, and use it largely in their training programs. The standard is easy to handle, stable and safe when properly flown. The wingspan for standard class craft is limited to 49.2 feet (15 meters).

Sports class are often low-performance gliders that have been modified for competition. Many are "homebuilts," perhaps constructed in someone's garage, or made a club project. A few may be made from purchased plans, or partially assembled kits available from various manufacturers. Regardless of origin, all gliders must be thoroughly checked,

The standard class 15-meter wingspan glider is often used in competitive sailplaning. *Schweizer Aircraft Corp.*

An airborne high-performance open class sailplane is a thing of beauty. *Schempp-Hirth*

tested, and certified by the FAA before being allowed to fly.

Sports class gliders are very popular in competition. They can be handicapped according to their individual performance capabilities in order to make the competition fair and even. In any meet you will find sports class sailplanes entered in such fun events as spot landing contests where the one who touches down on or nearest to a spot marked on the airstrip is the winner. They also are highly maneuverable when used for simulated bomb drops where you bombard some ground target with water balloons or flour bombs. They, indeed, participate in any other entertaining and challenging events that glider pilots are prone to think of. This may include such aerobatics as loops, rolls, and assorted other flying gyrations that gliders are capable of performing, but that are best left to the experts.

You come then to the third, or open, class gliders. These are the long-winged, streamlined, usually fiberglass sailplanes. They are lightweight and soar gracefully on the barest amount of available lift. They are also expensive. Whereas you can purchase a standard class sailplane for about the price of a compact automobile, one of the high-performance, fully instrumented fiberglass or carbon fiber beauties can run up to forty thousand dollars or so. Most records are held by such sailplanes, some of which have wingspans of around 80 feet (approximately 24 meters). Such gliders are a job to fly and a joy to behold.

But the cost of a glider or the length of its wing is not the way to measure the magnificence of soaring. Once you have learned to fly a glider—any glider—there are no limits to the pleasures and challenges that you get from your new-found skills in the air. Indeed, you have learned to woo the winds, play among the clouds, and look down upon the world from the lofty domain where hawks and eagles fly.

Glossary

Aerodynamics: The study of motion within the earth's atmosphere.

Aeronautics: The science of flight.

Aero tow: To tow a glider aloft with a powered airplane.

Aileron: A hinged tab on the wing's trailing edge, used in turning.

Airspeed indicator (ASI): The instrument that measures speed in relation to the surrounding air.

Airworthiness certificate: A record of aircraft inspections.

Altimeter: The cockpit instrument that measures aircraft's altitude.

Altocumulus: Puffy clouds at high altitudes with shadowy portions.

Angle of attack: The nose-up tilt of an aircraft.

Axis (plural, **axes**): A straight theoretical line around which an object rotates.

Barograph: An instrument that traces various aspects of a flight.

Base leg: The crosswind portion of the landing pattern approaching the runway from the side.

Canopy: The enclosure over a cockpit.

Center of gravity (CG): The point at which the aircraft is in complete balance.

Certified Flight Instructor (CFI): The highest glider pilot rating.

Clear the sky: To look carefully for other aircraft around you.

Cloud street: A lineup of cumulus clouds enabling a pilot to hop from one to another on a lengthy flight.

Cockpit: Where the pilot sits.

Commercial pilot: A fully licensed professional pilot.

Compass: The navigational instrument that tells direction.

Control stick: The cockpit column or yoke that activates elevator and ailerons.

Crew: Those who assist in glider operations and retrieval.

Cross-country: An extended flight.

Cumulonimbus: Towering thunderhead clouds.

Cumulus (cu): A puffy cloud of condensing vapor that usually forms atop a column of rising warm air.

Derig: To dismantle a glider.

Downwind leg: The normal downwind entry into a three-sided landing pattern.

Drag: A frictional force that hinders movement through the air.

Elevator: The horizontal hinged tail surface that controls a glider's pitch.

Empennage: A tail assembly usually made up of fin, rudder, stabilizer, and elevator.

Federation Aeronautique Internationale (FAI): The world governing body of flying contests, and keeper of world records.

Federal Aviation Agency (FAA): The official controlling agency of aviation in the United States.

Federal Aviation Regulations (FARs): The rules by which fliers must abide.

Fin: The fixed vertical tail surface that provides directional stability.

Final approach: The final leg of the landing pattern that lines up with the runway.

Flaps: The hinged portions of the wing, inboard from the ailerons, that alter lift and drag characteristics.

Flare (round out): To flatten out the glider just before landing.

Fuselage: The aircraft's body.

Glide: To descend slowly in the surrounding air.

Glider (sailplane): An engineless winged aircraft.

Gliderport: An airfield for gliders.

Glide ratio: See **L/D**.

Gravity: The natural force pulling everything toward the earth's center.

High tow: When a glider holds position just above the tow-plane's wake.

Horizon: The line where sky and earth meet.

Hypoxia: A physical illness caused by insufficient oxygen.

Land out: An off-field landing where there is no established airport.

Lateral axis: A theoretical line passing from wingtip to wingtip.

L/D: The ratio of *lift* to *drag*. A 20:1 L/D (lift over drag) means the aircraft can glide twenty feet forward for each foot of lost altitude.

Lee wave: An upwelling of air just downwind of a ridge or mountain.

Lift: Rising air currents strong enough to support a glider; also the upward force generated by an aerodynamically shaped wing.

Logbook (log): An FAA-required record of each pilot's operations.

Longitudinal axis: A theoretical center line from nose to tail of the aircraft.

Meteorology: The science of weather.

Motorglider: A self-propelled sailplane that needs no towing.

National Aeronautics Association (NAA): The agency designated by the FAI to govern and administer flying contests in the United States.

Ornithopter: Unsuccessful wing-flapping machines intended to enable people to fly like birds.

Pitch: The up or down movement of the aircraft's nose.

Pitot tube: An exposed open-ended air tube that supplies atmospheric pressure to operate certain cockpit instruments.

Preflight: To inspect and prepare the glider for flight.

Private pilot: A flier licensed to carry passengers, but not for hire.

Red line: A red warning mark on the airspeed indicator beyond which it is unsafe to fly.

Retrieve: To track down and return a glider that lands out.

Ridge wind: Wind that ricochets up a slope or cliff.

Roll: Rotation around the longitudinal axis.

Rotor: Dangerous swirling air circulating beneath a lee wave.

Rudder: An upright hinged surface that controls yaw and helps guide the aircraft.

Rudder pedals: Foot pedals used to control the rudder.

Sailplane: See **Glider**.

Sink: Atmospheric conditions that cause a glider to lose altitude faster than is normal.

Soar: To fly without power and without loss of altitude.

Soaring Society of America (SSA): A division of NAA designated to help oversee glider activity in the United States.

Solo: To fly alone.

Spin: A spiraling nosedown aerobatic maneuver.

Spoiler: A movable braking device that disturbs the airflow across the wing to increase drag and spoil part of the wing's normal lift.

Stabilizer: The rigid horizontal tail surface that provides pitch stability.

Stall: To lose wing lift and forward motion, causing the aircraft to fall.

Stratus: A flat cloud.

Student pilot: A glider pilot in training.

Task: A glider pilot's mission for the day.

Thermal: Air rising from a heated surface, or pushed upward by a cold front or other atmospheric condition.

Thermaling: The art of flying within thermals.

Thrust: Forward-directed force.

Towplane (tug): The aircraft used to tow a glider aloft.

Trailing edge: The rear edge of wing or stabilizer.

Trim tab: A small movable device on the elevator used to keep the glider flying level with minimal pilot effort.

Turn and bank indicator: An instrument that detects slips and skids. The simple yaw string does the same thing.

Variometer (vario): A sensitive and important instrument that quickly registers the rate of lift or sink.

Vertical axis: A theoretical line sticking straight up through the aircraft's center of gravity.

Vertical stabilizer: See **Fin**.

Winch: A drum-and-cable device used to launch gliders.

Wind sock: A ground-based weather vane-like device that indicates the direction of the wind.

Yaw: A wagging, side-to-side movement of the aircraft's nose.

Yaw string: A simple, short piece of yarn anchored in the airstream that indicates whether the glider is flying straight ahead or yawing to the side.

Information Sources

Soaring Society of America (SSA)
P.O. Box E
Hobbs, NM 88241
(publishes *Soaring* magazine and will provide list of wide variety of books, publications, and soaring items, including *American Soaring Handbook*, ten separate training course booklets dealing with all phases of gliders and soaring)

Ridge Soaring, Inc.
R.D. Julian, PA 16844
(issues brochure listing a broad selection of equipment, publications, etc.)

National Soaring Museum
R.D. 3, Harris Hill
Elmira, NY 14903
(a great place to visit)

Books for Further Reading

Soaring by Carter Ayres
Lerner Publications, 1986

The Joy of Soaring by Carle Conway
Soaring Society of America, 1969

Half Mile Up Without an Engine by Robert Gannon
Prentice-Hall, 1982

Glider Basics: From First Flight to Solo by Tom Knauff
Northcut, Allen & Gilmore, 1982

Go Fly a Sailplane by Linda and Ray Morrow
Atheneum, 1981

Beginning Gliding by Derek Piggott
Barnes & Noble, 1975

Schweizer Soaring School Manual
Schweizer Aircraft Corp., Elmira, NY 14902

The Art and Technique of Soaring by Richard Wolters
McGraw-Hill, 1971

The World of Silent Flight by Richard Wolters
McGraw-Hill, 1979

Standard American Soaring Signals

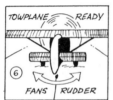

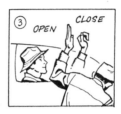

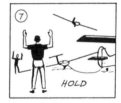

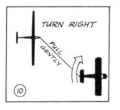

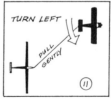

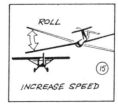

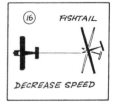

Awards and Notices of Achievement

A Emblem

Preflight to solo.
Complete course of preflight checks and operations.
Knowledge of safety rules and FAA regulations.
Dual flying instruction, followed by oral exam and preparation for and completion of first solo gliding flight.

B Emblem

Soaring skill.
Solo flight of at least 5 minutes' duration above low point after release, or 30 minutes' duration after release by aero tow from altitude of 2,000 feet.
Plus ever-increasing knowledge of sailplaning functions.

C Emblem

Cross-country preparation.
Have two hours minimum solo time.
Dual practice including thermal, ridge, and wave soaring techniques.
Glider assembly, tracking, and retrieval crew experience.
Solo flight of at least 30 minutes' duration above

low release point, or 60 minutes' duration after release from an aero tow altitude of 2,000 feet. Become a serially numbered member of the soaring society.

Silver or
Golden C

Flight of at least 5 hours.
Flight of not less than 31.2 miles (50 kilometers) in a straight line.
Gain of at least 3,280 feet (1,000 meters) above point of release.

Silver or
Golden C

Flight of at least 5 hours.
Flight of not less than 187 miles (300 kilometers).
Gain of at least 9,843 feet (3,000 meters) above point of release.

A Diamond is earned by completing any of the following tasks:

Diamond C

Flight to a preselected and announced goal and back of not less than 187 miles (300 kilometers).

Flight of not less than 310.7 miles (500 kilometers) in a straight line, over a triangular course, on a return trip, or as a dog leg with one turning point.

Gain of 16,404 feet (5,000 meters) above point of release.

Index